THE ULTIMATE GUIDE TO

Witchcraft

A Modern-Day Guide to
Making Magick

Anjou Kiernan

FAIR WINDS

Inspiring | Educating | Creating | Entertaining

Brimming with creative inspiration, how-to projects, and useful information to enrich your everyday life, Quarto Knows is a favorite destination for those pursuing their interests and passions. Visit our site and dig deeper with our books into your area of interest: Quarto Creates, Quarto Cooks, Quarto Homes, Quarto Lives, Quarto Drives, Quarto Explores, Quarto Gifts, or Quarto Kids.

First Published in 2020 by Fair Winds Press, an imprint of The Quarto Group, 100 Cummings Center, Suite 265-D, Beverly, MA 01915, USA. T (978) 282-9590 F (978) 283-2742 QuartoKnows.com

Fair Winds Press titles are also available at discount for retail, wholesale, promotional, and bulk purchase. For details, contact the Special Sales Manager by email at specialsales@quarto.com or by mail at The Quarto Group, Attn: Special Sales Manager, 100 Cummings Center, Suite 265-D, Beverly, MA 01915, USA.

24 23 22 21 20   1 2 3 4 5

ISBN: 978-1-59233-929-7

Digital edition published in 2019
eISBN: 978-1-63159-834-0

Library of Congress Cataloging-in-Publication Data

Names: Kiernan, Anjou, author.
Title: The ultimate guide to witchcraft : a modern-day guide to making
  magick / Anjou Kiernan.
Description: Beverly, MA : Fair Winds Press, 2020. | Includes bibliographical references and index. | Summary: "Written by Anjou Kiernan-named "One of the Magical Women You Should be Following on Instagram," by Refinery 29-The Ultimate Guide to Witchcraft is a beginner's guide to the practice of witchcraft, providing a complete toolkit for cultivating your own practice. Magic is not for the select few. We all have the ability to connect to the power of the natural and supernatural worlds to support our intentions. Blending ancient practices with modern context, this guide gives aspiring witches a practical, easy-to-follow path through the study of natural witchcraft and ritual. Whether you are looking to commune with spirits across the veil, need an amulet for protection, wish to build your magical apothecary, create a grimoire, or curate a crystal collection for vibrational work, this guide will empower and inform your craft. Learn how to harness the power of the moon, elements, and seasons to amplify your spells and divination work. Whether for personal development or spiritual enlightenment, The Ultimate Guide to Witchcraft is the perfect guide for teaching you how to tap into your own magic and apply its alchemy to your life"-- Provided by publisher.
Identifiers: LCCN 2019024820 | ISBN 9781592339297 | ISBN 9781631598340
  (eISBN)
Subjects: LCSH: Witchcraft.
Classification: LCC BF1566 .K468 2020 | DDC 133.4/3--dc23
LC record available at https://lccn.loc.gov/2019024820

Design and Page Layout: Laura Mcfadden Design Inc.
Photography: Anjou Kiernan
Illustration: Anjou Kiernan except pages 3, 8, 12, 15, 17, 23, 29, 44, 49, 52, 76, 77, 104, 107, 112, 137, 151, 158, 159, 161, 163, 170, 171, 180, 187, 189 are shutterstock

Printed in China

To Colton, who creates magick
wherever he goes

CONTENTS

CHAPTER 1

THE MODERN APPROACH TO WITCHCRAFT

Witchcraft is the belief that the universe weaves an indescribable magick through the stars. It is the knowledge that the linear thought processes of human consciousness are but one facet of our existence. By its very definition, witchcraft is not meant to be confining or rigid, stagnant or stale. It is meant to encompass the vastness of our experience, including that which we have yet to understand.

Witchcraft listens to the groaning of the trees, the howling of the winds, and the whispers of spirits across the veil. It changes and grows with our needs and the needs of the world around us. In its very essence, witchcraft is the relationship that we cultivate with the unseen forces of nature. This book will help you develop your own relationship with the magickal forces that abound by guiding you through a modern approach to natural witchcraft that is based on ancient practices. From harnessing the power of the Moon to seeking answers from beyond, it will empower you to create your own personal brand of magick that resonates with the universe.

The Origin of Witchcraft

In the beginning, there was only witchcraft. Tens of thousands of years before recorded history began, hunter-gatherers performed rituals under skies twinkling with mystery. The Lascaux cave paintings from the Paleolithic period, created by artists who were under the influence of trance dances, depict shamans, hunting rituals, and animal figures. Mother goddess figurines and a horned god—figures prevalent in Wicca and other duotheistic neopagan religions—appeared, alongside evidence of ceremonial burials, cremations, and ritual artifacts.

As these prehistoric societies evolved, they formed cults and made sacrifices in conjunction with Sun and Moon magick. Thought to represent the birth of pre-Christian religion in old Europe, these cults are the basis for many modern witchcraft-centered religions. While the term "witch" did not appear until much later in the Old Testament (1 Samuel), early humans certainly practiced what we would consider today to be witchcraft. Witchcraft's evolution, like much of human history, was shaped by the ebb and flow of cultures throughout the various regions of the world. You will find elements of Hinduism, Christianity, and other ancient religions in modern pagan practices, and vice versa, as a result of invasions, trade routes, and even documentation of witch trials. Though pagan practices have historically been suppressed by patrifocal monotheism, resurgent beliefs in the old ways and the neopagan revival have, in many ways, opened the doors for the reclamation of ancient pagan practices, and have helped to incorporate them into the modern practice.

Wicca, Witchcraft, and Religion

One of the prevailing misconceptions about modern witchcraft is that to call yourself a witch, you must be Wiccan. Wicca is actually a contemporary pagan religion developed by retired British civil servant Gerald Brosseau Gardner in 1954, and it derives many of its tenets and rituals from global pre-Christian paganism. Although Gardner referred to it only as Witchcraft (or "the Craft") in his writings, it was dubbed "Wicca" after it began to spread from England to North America.

Both then and now there has been much controversy surrounding Gardner, particularly regarding his fixation on ritual sex and nudism and an increasing focus on the God over the Goddess. Many traditions split off from this original form of "Gardnerian Wicca," and most of them adapted or transformed the basic tenets that Gardner set forth into forms of Wicca that were based around a particular ancient culture or around a matriarchal focus.

While Wicca and its traditions are immeasurable in their value to the witching community, it is possible to incorporate the same magickal practices and elements that originated in pre-Christian paganism into our own practice without subscribing to any witchcraft-based religion. This is what is known as secular witchcraft. By simply focusing on creating magick with the natural world, we can open our practice beyond the limitations of religion.

Thankfully, witchcraft has continued to dissociate itself from the negative connotations that have plagued it in the past. Nowadays many people who adhere to mainstream religions also identify as witches. After all, there is no rule stating that a witch must refute the supreme beings that belong to Christianity and other theistic religions. When it comes down to it, witchcraft and theistic religions share the same core belief—that there are supernatural forces at work in the world and that cultivating a relationship with them is the underlying purpose of our existence. Once we understand this, it becomes clear that witchcraft can peacefully coexist alongside organized religion.

Magic Versus Magick

Like most concepts in this book, whether or not to make a distinction between the words *magic* and *magick* is a choice that every witch can make for themselves. While magic has been associated with everything from ancient shamanistic journeys to pulling rabbits out of hats, *magick* has been used only in the practice of occultism.

Thought to have first been publicized in the sixteenth century by Heinrich Cornelius Agrippa in his *Three Books of Occult Philosophy*, and later by Aleister Crowley, a Victorian occultist who was the main influence for Gardnerian Wicca, the term *magick* has come to represent the kind of modern craft practiced with an authentic belief in the ability to transform natural laws. So, with the increasing popularization of witchcraft, many witches have felt the need to reclaim the true practice of occultism and have chosen to adopt the altered spelling as a result. Because this guide leads you on a ritual-based path through natural witchcraft, we also use the term *magick* in the pages that follow. That said, you do not have to earn the right to participate in, or be born into, magick. It is not the one true path, nor is it exclusive. It is simply there to claim if you choose it.

FAMOUS GRIMOIRES IN HISTORY

The Sworn Book of Honorius is thought to be one of the oldest medieval grimoires, appearing in manuscripts since the thirteenth century. Its ninety-three chapters detail necromancy and magickal operations as well as unique rituals for finding treasure or catching thieves. It is said to have been compiled from an ancient magicians' conference that sought to preserve magick in the face of persecution.

The Key of Solomon, a medieval book of magick, dates back to the fourteenth or fifteenth century and contains spells and incantations to invoke spirits and demons. Purification, invisibility, astrological timing, and magickal tools are also detailed within the ceremonial rituals.

Three Books of Occult Philosophy by Renaissance scholar Heinrich Cornelius Agrippa were published in the sixteenth century and discuss ritual magick using the elements, astrology, alchemy, herbs, charms, sigils, and divination. This magickal trilogy is said to be the basis for Western occultism and modern witchcraft.

The Magus by British occultist Francis Barrett was published in the early nineteenth century and is a comprehensive handbook of occult and ceremonial magick. It was compiled from rare, magickal texts such as those listed previously. It is considered to be one of the most important texts in the Victorian occult revival.

What is Magick?

So what exactly, then, is magick? When we harness the power of the stars and align ourselves with the natural world, what is it that we cultivate? By definition, magick is the manipulation of the unseen forces of nature. But in the context of your intangible experiences in the world, it is so much more. It is the way a path seems to open up to you when you listen to the trees. It is the intuition you take into the unknown after convening with the Moon.

It is the mantra that heals the wound in your heart. Ultimately, magick is the harnessing of the subtle energies of the universe to bring about change. What it will change, and the extent of that change, is entirely dependent on you, the practitioner.

Magick is neutral: It is neither good nor evil. It is only what you make of it. However, there are two categories that craftwork—the practice of witchcraft—generally falls into. *Constructive* magick is that which seeks increase, growth, or to bring something to the practitioner: new love, prosperity, career advancement, or a bountiful harvest, for instance. *Destructive* magick, on the other hand, is used to decrease or destroy. While destructive magick has often been associated with black magick, it is not malefic in itself. In fact, there are many ways in which a benevolent witch can use it. Banishing addictions, breaking hexes or curses, cleansing or protecting sacred spaces, or releasing toxic people or energy are all examples of how destructive magick can be used for good.

Sympathetic magick is another modality of magick that can be considered when planning rituals. When we visualize a desired outcome of our ritual, symbolically imitate the effect we are seeking, use artifacts of a person or object to work our spells, or use symbolism in any way (for example, using the color red to represent passion), we are practicing sympathetic magick. Poppets, distance healing or protection spells, using honey jars to attract prosperity, candle magick, elemental or planetary magick, or any spells that use symbolism to effect change are included in this magickal modality. (It is important to remember that it is always wise to obtain permission beforehand when using sympathetic magick to benefit another person.)

While you may have heard that practitioners of white magick, or "white witches," practice magick only to benefit the greater good, the truth is that it is unrealistic to expect any practitioner of magick to be wholly selfless. If we are to excel as healers, diviners, and wise ones, then we require a certain level of ritualistic self-care to feed our magick. In modern witchcraft, we consider white magick simply to be that magick that aspires to effect only positive changes. When you are thinking about the types of rituals or spells you wish to add to your magickal repertoire, always remember that the type of energy that you release is bound to come back to you as part of the natural order of things. Whether you refer to it as the Rule of Three, karma, or another variant, it is the defining line between white and black magick. Do not be fooled into thinking that black magick refers only to destructive magick. While the transition from the former to the latter is certainly an easy one, black magick is just as capable of using constructive spells to achieve its ends. The movie-style "love spell," for instance, is an example of constructive black magick. Although coaxing someone to fall in love with you seems harmless enough, bending anyone's emotions against their will is not the type of energy that you want returning to you. As a practitioner of white magick, you would instead focus on opening your heart, increasing your attraction, brightening your aura, and letting love come to you. This is the subtle, but very important, distinction between white and black magick.

Natural Witchcraft

Like those who practice it, witchcraft comes in many forms. If you are a natural or eclectic witch—that is, you do not conform to any prescribed type of witchcraft or religion—you are not required to follow the doctrines set forth by this or any other book. This information is meant to be a guide for your practice, and you may choose to incorporate all of it, or merely bits and pieces of it.

This book is not religious in nature, but it is a composite of many magickal practices and much arcane knowledge. Modern witchcraft is the evolution of thousands of years of supernatural exploration, so it is only natural that it embraces magick from across time and space. It is important to note here, however, that while a witch is free to personalize their craft, great care should be taken that ceremonies belonging to a culture-specific religion outside of their own are not appropriated. While Voodoo and Native American spiritual practices certainly possess many intriguing concepts, the way in which these religions have been romanticized over the years has devalued the cultures that hold them sacred. There are lengthy journeys one must take in each path, some into which one must be initiated or born. As we make our own way through the wonderful world of witchcraft, we must respect the sacred rites of religions outside our own and ensure that we are not encroaching on them.

In the past, natural witchcraft was referred to as folk magick or *low magick*. Although some ceremonial magicians have perpetuated the claim that "low" refers to low-vibrational magick or magick without ritual, this is not the case. While folk magick can certainly make quick work of spells and charms, there is no more magick in a perfectly pronounced Latin chant than in a fully empowered witch who is deeply in tune with nature. Low magick has always been considered the magick of the common people, of the farmers of the "lowlands," where the term is thought to have originated. But it is also a sacred magick, as ancient as witchcraft itself. It draws from the very elements that form our cosmos in a close connection with nature. Ceremonial magick, on the other hand, has historically been the craft of the educated—those who were elevated both in terms of social status and intellect. It has been said that while folk magicians harness energy that is already present in nature—the energy that vibrates in herbs, crystals, and other elements—ceremonial magicians harness energy that has never been touched. To put it another way, if low magick harnesses the power of the Earth, high magick harnesses the power of the Sun. Is one better or more powerful than the other? No. When we look at the elements of nature, we will see that the four physical elements—earth, air, water, and fire—in balance comprise the path to ascension. All biases aside, high and low magick are merely *different* methods of harnessing the same ascended energy. As you will see, there are almost limitless ways to empower your magick. Whether you do so in complex ceremonies or in the belly of the elements is up to you. But rituals need not be complex to be effective.

"NATURAL WITCHCRAFT THEREFORE IS THAT, WHICH CONSIDERING WELL THE STRENGTH AND FORCE OF NATURAL AND CELESTIAL BEINGS, AND WITH GREAT CURIOSITY, LABORING TO DISCOVER THEIR HIDDEN AFFECTIONS, PRODUCES INTO OPEN ACT THE HIDDEN AND CONCEALED POWERS OF NATURE."
—Heinrich Cornelius Agrippa

Ritual-Based Practice

For some witches, incorporating magick into their lives is as simple as setting an intention for the day, casting a quick spell, or pulling a tarot card. For others, the ritual itself is what empowers their magick. And for others still, it is a combination of both. While simple, everyday magick can be a great asset for the witch low on time, money, or energy, this book will focus on rituals as a way of connecting with the world and wielding its power.

Rituals, as previously discussed, have been a part of witchcraft and the human experience since prehistoric times. They have been performed by shamans in the solace of caves and in cults under the light of the Full Moon. So, whether you choose to perform magick alone as a solitary witch, in groups or circles, as part of a pagan coven, or in a combination of the above may depend on the specific ritual you are performing. Some witches who perform solitary magick for most of their practice will take part in a monthly Full Moon ritual circle to amplify their powers during this important time. Others may belong to a coven but perform solitary rituals in the comfort of their own homes. Finding the best way to empower *your* magick is the key to achieving a reciprocal relationship with the universe.

CHAPTER 2

EMPOWERING YOUR CRAFT

Your magic grows inside you from the moment you are born. It slumbers, waiting for you to cradle it in your arms and release its cry into the wilds. Many may lure you with promises to raise your magick and provide you with successful spells and rituals, but only you—and you alone—can wield your magick. Empowering yourself is the first step in witchcraft, and, in some ways, it is the *only* step, since everything you will learn on your journey is but to aid your empowerment. Giving yourself the tools, the energy, and, most importantly, the space to grow your magick is hard work, but the payoff is immeasurable: Once you begin to nurture your craft, your craft will nurture you.

Energizing Your Magick

The Body: It is no secret that to take care of others, you must first take care of yourself. The same applies to your magick. Nurturing the physical body is crucial to building the energy required to create high-vibrational magick. Our bodies operate as a conduit for our magick, and without it we are but tetherless spirits floating in space.

Diet, exercise, sleep, health, and mood all play a role in optimizing the ability of the body to provide a sacred space in which magick can reside. Our bodies have an equilibrium that can often be maintained by observation. Closely honoring and working with your physical body is an excellent way to become intimate with its own individual version of equilibrium and finding that "sweet spot" can be incredibly transforming for your

practice. Diet alterations, yoga and meditation, sleep and dream work, and mood-boosting rituals can all help to bring you some balance. Often, a simple ritual bath is enough to reset your mood and cleanse you of any negative energy that you may be harboring.

SELF-LOVE RITUAL BATH

❧

To be used in bringing contentment with one's self. Best performed under the New Moon.

1 Cleanse the area around your bath. Begin to run the water.

2 Place rose quartz, clear quartz, and amethyst around the rim of the bathtub. Alternate the crystals with white and pink candles. If you like, carve a symbol into the candles such as a swan (for awakening to your true self and beauty) or a series of words such as "trust," "love," "self," and "rise."

3 Place 1 tablespoon (18 g) of pink Himalayan salt, 1 tablespoon (18 g) of Epsom salt, rose petals, hibiscus petals, and some of the crystals into the bath water. You can also include ten drops of plant oils, such as rose, jasmine, geranium, sandalwood, sweet orange, and bergamot.

4 Once the bath is full, gently step into the water and relax. Place a piece of rose quartz in the center of your chest. Put one hand on your heart and tune into your heartbeat (if you have trouble feeling your heartbeat, press two fingers into the pulse point on your neck and keep your right hand on your heart). If you like, time the following chant to each thump: "I am becoming."

5 Visualize a gentle light softly emanating from your heart. With each thump, it spreads outward until it illuminates the entire bath and turns the water a rosy pink.

6 When you are finished with your bath, apply an anointing oil made from sweet almond oil infused with dried rose petals or rosebuds, and any combination of the above plant oils, to extend the effects of the ritual.

The Spirit: Was there a time when you ascended to a higher energy level without knowing it? Perhaps you sat at a waterfall or a bubbling stream and listened. You listened for so long that you no longer felt you were of the Earth. Colors became brighter and the pace of everything around you slowed down so that the details of the rushing water became unnaturally crisp.

Or perhaps it was late at night, and you closed your eyes just as the Moon began to set. Sleep evaded you even as the clock ticked on and on, so you decided to try the progressive muscle relaxation trick you learned in yoga class. You gently tensed your muscles from your head down to your toes, relaxing each as you traveled down your center. Then, in a moment of unnatural bliss, you began to float . . . You weren't asleep just yet, but your body no longer felt connected to the bed.

When you are able to shed the restraints of your physical body, your energetic body—your etheric or astral body—takes over. It connects you to the universal life force all around you and draws energy from it to feed your magick. As you gain more and more energy, your aura, or the field of astral energy surrounding your physical body, extends outward. In natural witchcraft, the breadth and quality of your aura is a good indicator of the results you can expect from your rituals. High energy yields high-vibrational magick; low energy yields low-vibrational magick. So how do we raise our energy? How do we consciously take hold of those random and elusive moments of ascension?

As witches, we are blessed with the inherent knowledge that there are no such things as inanimate objects. A study performed by Swiss psychologist Jean Piaget in 1930 revealed that young children, unburdened by the mental constraints and learned biases of adulthood,

believe that the Moon knows the course of its travels, that rocks sense pain, and that clouds have intentions. Similarly, when you convene with nature, you tap into the energy of every tree in the forest or every grain of sand in the desert. Coaxing this energy out, however, is something that requires a bit of craftwork on your part, which can range from performing a simple meditation ritual in your backyard to calling upon the elements as you gaze upon a natural wonder.

If you have limited access to nature or simply prefer to work indoors, it is possible to bring nature to you. Filling your space with plants, crystals, feathers, water features, and other artifacts of the Earth can help you connect with the elements in the comfort of your own home. As witches, we can often become consumed by the idea that we must be out in nature to gather magick. In doing so, we forget that our bodies themselves are a natural product of the universe. Astronomer Carl Sagan famously said, "The nitrogen in our DNA, the calcium in our teeth, the iron in our blood, the carbon in our apple pies were made in the interiors of collapsing stars. We are made of starstuff." Truly, even without access to the outside world, you can still draw magick from within.

MAGIC-AWAKENING CHANT

To be used to energize the magick within.
Best performed under a Full Moon.

1 Find a quiet space that you feel comfortable in.

2 Close your eyes and clear your mind. Focus on a silhouette of your standing body on a black background.

3 Now envision a tiny point of light emanating from the center of your silhouette's pelvic area. Focus on your magick as that point of light and imagine that as your magick awakens, the light gets bigger and bigger, swelling and swelling until it takes over your entire field of vision.

4 Imagine glowing letters appearing in the center of the light. What do they say? With your eyes still closed, gently begin to vocalize the letters or word. Begin quietly articulating each letter. Slowly raise the volume until you can feel the letters or word vibrating throughout your entire body.

5 Open your eyes. Make a mental note of the word, and keep it as your energizing chant for future rituals.

Discovering Your Personal Brand of Magick

While energizing your magick can bring you much power, it is important to know how you will best wield it. Witches can draw energy from their environments in a number of ways, and what may speak to one witch may not speak to another. Have you considered where your magick comes most alive? Is it deep in the forest, as you seek the wisdom of the trees? Or perhaps it is in the kitchen, as you transform ingredients into a meal that nourishes body and spirit? Understanding the nature of your magick in this way can help you along your journey. The following list describes some of the common paths on which you might consider traveling:

Cottage Witch

When I think of the cottage witch, I imagine a tidy little stone house on a small homestead down in a bog. Have you read *The Witch of Blackbird Pond* by Elizabeth George Speare? If so, you'll be familiar with the character of Hannah Tupper, who would most likely be considered a cottage witch. Often a solitary practitioner, this witch has deep ties to the land and finds magick in every crevice in the walls of the home. The shelves are neatly stocked with dried herbs and, perhaps, animal parts such as bones, antlers, or snakeskin from a small herd of livestock or sustenance trapping. The cottage witch's land provides sustenance through cultivation of livestock and gardens. Like a kitchen witch, the cottage witch takes great care in preparing meals and will craft them to nourish the body as well as the spirit. Cleanliness and organization are of the utmost importance to the cottage witch, as the entire home and property is considered to be sacred. Typical ritual magick for the cottage witch might include floor sweeps and cleansing sprays, protection spells, animism, charms, animal telepathy, faerie and sprite magick, basic herbalism, knot-tying magick, water scrying, and baking spells. Animal guides such as cats, dogs, hummingbirds, and livestock are commonly called upon.

Forest Witch

Deep in the woods, the forest witch dwells with the will-o'-wisps and animal kin. Those who embark on the wooded path know the language of the ancient trees and the source of each scar on their bark. The talents of insects and arachnids are integral parts of their practice, too, and found specimens may line their walls and shelves, along with pinecones, leaves, bark, moss, and lichen. The forest witch often maintains an outdoor altar and connects with the element of each tree species and the life force that moves within the streams and rivers. Mushrooms and forest flowers like lady slippers are of special interest to the forest witch. Wood carving, wand- and staff-making, root, bark, and berry tinctures, tree magick, animal telepathy, nature spirits, stream and river scrying, resin and sap alchemy, and sustenance hunting and fishing may all constitute typical ritual magick for the forest witch. Animal guides such as rabbits, squirrels, mice, owls, foxes, bears, wolves, and snakes are commonly called upon.

Green Witch

The green witch uses plants to heal the body and the spirit. With a background in herbalism, the green witch focuses on transforming nature into medicine, using an in-depth knowledge of botany to maintain an extensive medicinal and magickal herb garden. Composting and growth mediums may interest the green witch, as well as communicating with plants via light, music, and speech. Wild-crafting and foraging for beloved and new ingredients is a pleasurable—and sacred— daily task. A green witch is never without a local plant guide, a blade or scythe for cutting herbs, gloves to protect against stinging nettles, and a basket for collecting the day's bounty. Taxonomy and mycology might be of special interest to the green witch. A full apothecary cabinet of tonics, tinctures, elixirs, salves, balms, herb blends, and teas is the central focus of the home. Ritual magick for the green witch might include plant communication and spells for plant health, protective herbs, faerie magick, Moon-phase gardening, herb-dressed candles, herbal oils and sprays, healing potions and ointments, and tree magick. Animal guides commonly called upon are those that act as pollinators—butterflies, flies, birds, and squirrels—as well as the insects that turn the earth.

Hedge Witch

Steeped in the tradition of Old Europe and descended from *cunning folk* (the medieval practitioners of folk magick), the hedge witch rides the border (or *hedgerow*) between this realm and the next. Gaining knowledge from the spirit world takes precedence only slightly over the hedge witch's knowledge of medicinal and magickal herbs, particularly as they pertain to opening the

THE WELLINGTON WITCH LADDER

In the nineteenth century, a rope woven with feathers was found, along with six brooms and a chair, in the roof space of an old house in Wellington, Somerset, in southwest England. The rope had three strands through which cock feathers were twisted in crossways along its length and a loop at one end for hanging. Interviews with neighbors revealed that creating such an item was common practice in casting curses to dry up the milk of neighbors' cows or to cause death. They claimed that the old woman who had died in the house was likely a witch. The workmen who found the rope during demolition, however, indicated that the brooms were ridden by witches who climbed the ladder to cross the roof. Today, we use witches ladders for many different purposes by weaving in intentions or protection spells into the rope as part of benevolent knot or cord magick. Although it is not certain whether the original witch ladder had magickal intentions, we certainly use them in our practice today. The Wellington Witch Ladder now hangs in the court of the Pitt Rivers Museum in Oxford, England.

third eye and healing the senses. In the practice of wortcunning, nature is closely observed, and poisonous plants are carefully studied for their trance-inducing qualities. Alchemy, the ability to transform the ordinary into the extraordinary, is something the hedge witch prefers to do instead of relying on finely crafted tools. A simple walking staff, leather pouch, blade or scythe for cutting herbs, and a flask or horn for transporting potions might be all a hedge witch needs to work magick.

Although divinatory work may involve tarot cards, pendulums, or crystal balls, the hedge witch can do just as well scrying on a moonlit pond or throwing bones and reading tea leaves. Typical ritual magick for the hedge witch might include divination, dream magick and hedge riding (or astral travel), spirit communication, ancestor veneration, and herbalism. Animal guides such as ravens, crows, owls, and cats are commonly called upon.

Hearth Witch

Home is where the hearth is: This is the mantra of the hearth witch. With deep ties to family, the hearth witch focuses on the home and all the creatures in it. A cozy fire is always lit in the gathering room, which is filled with comfortable rugs and furniture. Comfort food such as stews, soups, bread, and mulled cider are often enjoyed in front of the roaring flames as the wind howls outside the heavily draped windows. Candles and lanterns decorate the hearth witch's many altars and draw warming energy into the home. Fire tools, buckets, and cauldrons are welcome additions to the hearth, as well as besoms (see page 34), which may be present in every room. Ancestors and lineage are everything to the hearth witch, and family photos may line the walls. The hearth's cleanliness is of great importance, as it is often used as the main altar and the source of connection for the family. Typical ritual magick for the hearth witch might include fire scrying; candle magick; ancestor veneration; herb-casting; fire purification spells; charm bags; threshold protection spells; knot-tying spells such as witches ladder; knitting, quilting, sewing; besom-making and family bonding. Animal guides such as cats, dogs, and winter hibernators are commonly called upon.

Kitchen Witch

There is magick in food, and the kitchen witch knows how to intricately weave it through each and every recipe. Meals are often laced with spells and include only the finest ingredients, which are chosen for their medicinal and metaphysical attributes. A small herb garden or window box and an expansive spice rack along with pot racks and a bevy of copper and cast iron pots and pans allow the kitchen witch to work edible alchemy. If crops or meat are not raised on the kitchen witch's land, foraging for plants, berries, and mushrooms or selecting local ingredients at the farmers' market might be a weekend routine. Wine- and beer-making as well as distillation may be part of the kitchen witch's repertoire. Counters and tables are sacred spaces and elaborate centerpieces are often crafted to honor the season or meal being presented. Typical ritual magick for the kitchen witch might include bread magick, tonics and potion-making, food spells and enchantments, symbolic food, tasseomancy, Moon phase and ritual meals, herb-dressed candles, salt protection spells, healing salves for cuts and burns, and cleaning rituals. Animal guides such as cats, dogs, birds, mice, rats, and raccoons are commonly called upon.

This is just a small sample of the paths available to the natural witch. In considering these, you may find that your own path does not lead you to any one of them—or you may feel a connection to all of them. That is perfectly okay! Many witches have a deeply personal relationship with their magick, and yours may shift according to the seasons, your unique needs, your family traditions, or your relationship with religion and deities. What is important is that you understand how *your* magick will be best used.

Preparing Your Sacred Space for Ritual

Just as there are many ways to perform rituals, there are many ways to prepare for them. At its core, ritual magick strives to achieve the goals that the practitioner sets forth. In this book, then, we will use the term "ritual" interchangeably with "spell," although spells are typically used within rituals to bring about a specific result.

Planning Your Ritual

The single most important thing you can do to prepare for your ritual is to have a clear focus, which is essential to directing your magick toward your goal and can help you to gather all the tools you will need beforehand. If divination is in your practice, it is a good idea to perform a tarot spread or other divinatory measure prior to your ritual to ensure that you are on the right track. Once you have developed a plan for your ritual, writing it down in your grimoire or witch's journal (see page 37) can help it to go smoothly.

Cleansing Your Space

Cleansing your sacred space is something that can be done as needed but is especially useful before a ritual. Smoke and fire have been used throughout history to purify land and prepare it for rebirth. The addition of plant oils helps to drive away unwanted insects and repel pathogens. Burning herbs such as sage, cedar, sweet grass, and lavender, as well as tree resins like copal, frankincense, and myrrh, can dispel even the most stubborn negative energies. Alternatively, you could use an herb-infused essential oil mist with any combination of the above, or cleansing crystals such as clear quartz, amethyst, or black tourmaline. Salt water, elemental water, or an herbal floor sweep can also help clear a space of stuck energy.

Also, cleansing your body and your aura is just as important as purifying your space, so a ritual bath or pass with any of the above could be part of your pre-ritual routine.

Cleansing Your Tools

Now that you have planned your ritual and cleansed your space, you can gather and cleanse your tools. This can be done by passing smoke from the before-mentioned herbs over the tools; by purifying them in fire or over the flame of a candle; by cleansing them in elemental water or salt water; by placing them in a bed of salt or herbs; or by passing a cleansing crystal over them.

Protecting Your Space

In preparing for a ritual, you may choose to define the area around you as sacred, meaning that it is protected from any unwanted outside energy that may compromise your ritual. Done in a variety of ways, common methods include casting a circle of white light around the space, placing candles or protective crystals around the space, or creating a physical protective barrier with salt or herbs.

When casting a circle, ensure that all of the items you will need for the ritual are within the circle before you begin. Using a wand, a crystal, a candle, or just your finger, cast a circle of protection around your space: Stand still in your space and spin around your axis, drawing a circle with your tool of choice. This circle will also help to draw in desired energy for your ritual. For additional protection or energy, you can sprinkle a circle of salt or herb water around your space. Rue and Florida Water are both excellent preparations for protecting your space from negative energy.

BASIC RITUAL PREPARATIONS

To be used prior to performing a ritual or spell.

1 In meditation or divination, focus on a particular goal you would like to manifest, such as self-love, increased confidence, or a promotion at work. Record this goal in your grimoire or journal. Write out any incantations, chants, or mantras that will help you focus your magick. Research the tools that might help you in your ritual and collect them. Include a closing for your ritual and consider creating a charm or token of your ritual to carry with you, stow under your pillow, or place on your altar to continue the effects of the ritual.

2 Choose a space that feels comfortable and energetic to you. This can be at your altar, at the base of your favorite tree, in the middle of a field, or anywhere else that speaks to you. Carefully light a bundle of sage and cedar until smoke begins to form. Slowly wave the bundle around your space and over your body, paying particular attention to your hands and third eye. When you are done, place the smoldering herb bundle facedown in a fireproof bowl.

3 Gather all of your ritual tools, including your grimoire and any candles, herbs, or ritual oils you may want to use. Lay them out on an altar cloth, blanket, or rug in front of you. Take your herb bundle and slowly pass the smoke over your tools. You can verbalize a simple intention, such as "I cleanse this space and prepare for ritual," or something more complex (in which case, be sure to write your intention out beforehand). Visualizing negative energy and impurities being stripped away from your tools can add to the effect.

4 Holding your ceremonial blade or wand, stand up behind your altar or tools. Raise the blade up in the air, close your eyes, and tilt your head up. Envision your aura meeting a bright white light coming down from the cosmos and entering the tip of your blade. As the light enters, it travels down the blade, down your arm, and along your body. You can speak a simple incantation such as, "The light of the universe and I become one," and then tilt your blade down to the earth and draw a circle around your space as you spin in a clockwise fashion. Visualize a ring of white light around your space closing at the point where you started, then open your eyes. Place the ritual blade back down on your altar cloth and begin your ritual. You can use the blade to open the circle at the close of your ritual so that your energy is no longer tied up in a space you are not using. This can be done in reverse—by drawing the circle in a counterclockwise fashion as you visualize the light returning through your blade.

Ritual Tools for the Natural Witch

The flickering of a candle flame, the dripping of wax on a glinting witch's blade as it carves protection symbols of an ancient origin . . . This evocative imagery is what many people think of when they imagine the magickal workings of the modern-day witch. Yes, witches' tools *can* be useful energy conduits that also add their own energy to the ritual. But, even in ritual magick, tools are not a requirement when practicing natural witchcraft.

With enough energy, you can manifest any goal that you put your magick to without external assistance. However, if you find yourself lacking focus or energy, or if you simply enjoy the additional energy that rituals tools bring, then they can certainly be of great use. Here are some tools you might find helpful in your practice:

Altar

A sacred space used for magickal workings, an altar is often created on a raised surface and comprises ritual tools and symbols that serve a particular intention. Altars can change with the seasons, honor certain deities or ancestors, or function as permanent workspaces. Many witches will have more than one altar throughout their homes to reflect their current magickal foci. Altar cloths can be used as protection from dirt and debris and as a symbolic addition to your altar or ritual.

Bell or Singing Bowl

The chime of a bell or the deep vibration of a singing bowl can help you to tune into and summon your energy before a ritual, or to call upon energies from beyond the veil. If you play a musical instrument, you could substitute it here: A single note or chord played repetitively can often calm the mind and channel your magick to the ritual at hand.

Besom

The traditional witch's broom that serves as a tool of purification and used only in ritual, the besom symbolically sweeps away negative energy before magickal work begins. The symbol of witches' legendary ability to fly, it can be used as a ritual tool for riding the hedges (see page 26). Besoms are typically crafted from an ash handle and birch twigs wrapped with willow branches.

Blade

A ceremonial sword or knife can be used in rituals to direct energy, or a utility knife can be used for cutting herbs and twine or carving symbols. Often, the ceremonial blade is only used ritually and is not intended to cut anything in the physical realm. When using a ceremonial blade, it may be helpful to include a handle or stone of protective qualities, like black tourmaline, black obsidian, or black onyx. The ritual utility blade is typically curved but can take any form, including that of a pocket knife. In the Wiccan religion, the ceremonial blade is called an athame, while the white-handled utility blade is called a boline.

Candles

An integral part of the witches' practice and a symbol of the Fire element. Candles can be used to purify both the air and your sacred space to add to the power of a particular ritual or to add ambiance and act as focal points—or they can be spells in and of themselves. They can be dressed with herbs and crystals, and carved with symbols in ritual. If the candle is made with natural ingredients, you may also use the melted wax as an anointing oil.

Crystals

Crystals are born deep within the Earth and carry unique vibrations with them. These vibrations can bolster your ritual work and amplify your magick as well as provide a beautiful centerpiece and focal point for your altar. Crystal grids can be used to amplify or direct energy in a ritual.

Divination Tools

Including dowsing pendulums, tarot cards, crystal balls, and runes, these tools are used to divine the future or explore the etheric realm. They can add symbolic focus to your ritual and/or provide you with guidance in your practice.

Elemental or Moon Water

A clean container of natural water that you have collected from rain, snow, a spring, or some other natural source is a great addition to your magickal toolkit. It can be used in elemental magick to cleanse your crystals and tools or for scrying. Moon water is elemental water that has been charged in a particular Moon phase. It can then be used in your magickal workings.

Fireproof Vessel

A fireproof bowl or cauldron, typically made of cast iron, abalone, ceramic, or soapstone is necessary for burning loose incense, herbs, or new moon intentions, or for making offerings.

Grimoire

Also known as a Wiccan Book of Shadows or a witch's journal, this is a workbook where you can record all of your rituals, spells, herbal recipes, or other any information that adds to your practice. You can make it as simple or as complex as you like. Binding parchment with leather cord, willow, or twine can be a magickal way of weaving a protection spell into your grimoire.

Herbs, Incense, and Salt

Loose items like herbs and incense can be burned in a fireproof bowl or sprinkled around your altar to cleanse and protect the space and to draw energy to your ritual. Salt is often employed as a barrier of protection and can be used to cast a circle of protection around your altar or sacred space.

Mortar and Pestle

A mortar and pestle can be kept specifically for grinding herbs, powders, and incense for magickal workings. While you can also use a coffee grinder or food processor, grinding your ingredients by hand can add energy and focus to your ritual.

Wand

Used in the same way as the ceremonial blade, a wand can be used to cast a circle of protection or to direct energy during a ritual. Crystals and symbols can be added to the wand to strengthen its abilities. A wand can be made from glass or from crystal, such as selenite, or it can be carved from sacred wood such as alder, ash, oak, rowan, or willow.

CHAPTER 3

MOON MAGICK

The Moon is so sacred, so undeniably present in our lives, that its power escapes almost no one. We watch it rise and fall each evening, its light reflecting on our meadows and oceans. Even a busy cityscape stands in awe of its illumination. Sometimes the Moon is so large, we feel like we could reach out and stroke its cratered face. Other times it is just a distant silver crescent hanging in the sky.

Whatever phase the Moon is in, there is no denying its pull on us. Of all the celestial bodies, the Moon is nearest to our planet and to our hearts, affecting our oceans and ever-flowing emotions. Happily, lunar astrology is one of the easiest ways to incorporate the magick of the cosmos into your practice. The Moon has a set cycle of phases, reliably changing its face as it travels through each of the zodiac constellations. Timing spells with the lunar calendar brings a synchronicity to our magick that rivals that of the elements. And yet, the Moon aligns with the elements, too. Water, the Moon's elemental ruler, ebbs and flows with its gravitational pull.

Timing Your Magick with the Moon

The changing lunar landscape has transformed the night sky every evening since the dawn of time. The Moon bestows upon us gravity that turns the tides; light that illuminates a path; and energy that feeds our magick. All of these gifts wax and wane with its lunation throughout the month in a cycle we call the lunar calendar.

The creation of the lunar calendar dates back to the Upper Paleolithic period in Europe, right around the same time of the earliest origins of witchcraft. Communing with the phases of the Moon is one of the most ancient examples of the practice of nature-based magick. Tapping into our ability to observe the Moon in the sky, like our ancestors in millennia past, can tell us a lot about how best to draw its power to our own practice.

After the New Moon conjunction with the Sun, the Moon is in a *waxing* phase, meaning that it is growing or increasing into a Full Moon. You can easily pick out a waxing moon in the sky by observing that the outside curvature of light is on the right. Two helpful mnemonics to help you remember this are "Bright on right, getting light" and "Waxing is maxing." When the Moon is decreasing from a Full Moon to a New Moon, it is *waning*, and the illuminated curvature will be on the left.

PLANTING A MOON GARDEN

One way to honor the night sky's brightest luminary is to plant a moon garden. In this lunar oasis, you can showcase plants that are best suited to the magick of the evening sky. Night-blooming plants such as evening primrose, moonflowers, nicotiana, datura, angel's trumpets, and night-blooming jasmine can bring high drama to the garden as they release their splendor at dusk. Flowers chosen for their fragrance, too, like lavender, gardenia, lilac, peonies, roses, and snowdrops, can create a sensual experience that plays to the Moon's emotional side. The addition of silvery foliage in the form of artemisia, juniper, and variegated hosta will weave a luminescent blanket upon which the moonlight can reflect. Together, these plants can provide a sacred ritual space in which to capture the beauty of the Moon and draw down its power. The space itself can be a simple arrangement of potted plants on a moonlit windowsill or an elaborate bed on the banks of a scrying pond. Adding water features or soothing nature sounds can make the space even more pleasant and attune you to the Moon's watery pull.

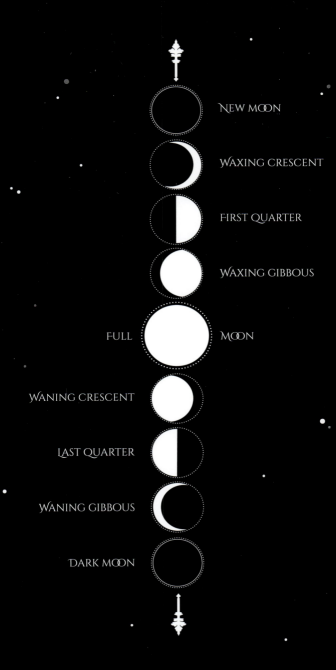

NEW MOON

WAXING CRESCENT

FIRST QUARTER

WAXING GIBBOUS

FULL   MOON

WANING CRESCENT

LAST QUARTER

WANING GIBBOUS

DARK MOON

Magickal Moon Phases

Each moon phase brings with it a unique energy that can empower our rituals. Although there are technically eight moon phases, we will focus on the four major phases and the Dark Moon as well as other magickally important moons.

New Moon

The New Moon is the very first appearance of the Waxing Crescent; it appears as a sliver of light in the sky. It is a time for new beginnings, business ventures, intention setting, and seed planting. Setting your goals within two days of the New Moon will ensure that they have ample time to grow during the waxing phase.

New Moon Bay Leaf Ritual *To be used in mani-festing intentions. Best performed under the New Moon in an outdoor space.*

1 Cleanse the air with sage (see page 31) and cast a protective circle of salt around you.

2 Sit in a comfortable and open position and meditate on an intention you would like to manifest.

3 Write this intention in a word or two on a bay leaf—which has the power to grant wishes—and read it aloud.

4 Burn the bay leaf in a fireproof vessel as you continue to chant your intention aloud. Burning the intention transforms it into elemental energy so that it can be incorporated into the universal force that abounds.

5 When the embers have cooled, blow the ashes into the wind, allowing it to carry your intention with it. Alternatively, make the ashes into a paste and use it to draw a symbol at the top of your abdomen (the solar plexus chakra). You could make a circle to represent the New Moon or draw a personal power sigil, since this area of your body is responsible for your inner strength.

Waxing Moon

The Waxing Moon appears to grow before our eyes, gaining brightness and girth as it increases from a Waxing Crescent to a First Quarter to a Waxing Gibbous. This phase is all about constructive magick and bringing positive things into our lives, such as love, money, fertility, career opportunities, and good health.

Full Moon

This is when the Moon's energy is the strongest. While this powerful phase can be used to amplify any spell, the Full Moon is especially useful for celebrations, cleansing and charging magickal tools and crystals, divination, spirit invocation, intuition, dream work, and hedge riding or astral projection.

Full Moon Water *To be used for creating lunar-charged water for magickal amplification. Best performed under a Full Moon.*

1 During moonrise, collect water from a fresh source such as a spring, stream, river, or rain in a clean glass bowl or jar. You may use purified water if you do not have access to a natural water source.

(To determine the time of moonrise in your region, look online or consult *The Old Farmer's Almanac*.)

2 Place the container in full view of the Moon's light, preferably in a safe spot outdoors. (A window will suffice, too.)

3 Place a clear quartz generator or moonstone in or around the container or on top of the lid to bring additional energy to the ritual and say a small intention, like "Charge this water with the full energy of the Moon."

4 Allow the water to charge for at least a few hours (but bring it indoors before sunrise) and bottle. Store in a cool, dark place.

5 Use the Moon water to anoint yourself and your tools in lunar rituals or moon circles; to charge crystals; in divination work such as scrying; or in dream work.

Waning Moon

From the Full Moon to the New Moon, the Moon is in a waning phase. During this time, it appears to decrease in size, and this is the ideal time to practice destructive magick—releasing what no longer serves you, ending toxic situations, quitting addictions, and releasing negativity.

Dark Moon

The Dark Moon occurs when the Sun and the Moon are in conjunction. During this liminal phase, the Moon is shrouded in darkness, hidden from the naked eye. Banishing and binding spells and deep introspection are best performed during the Dark Moon.

Only occurring at certain or rare times, the following moons provide powerful energies for magic making.

Blue Moon

Although there are generally 29 days in a lunar cycle, there are 365 days per year, which means that some years can have 13 Full Moons instead of 12. A Blue Moon is a Full Moon that occurs in a month that has already had a Full Moon. This powerful second Full Moon can be used to perform a spell that seems truly miraculous or to bring about something that, as they say, only happens "once in a blue moon."

Black Moon

A Black Moon is a second Dark Moon that occurs in the same month. This is an extremely powerful time for being still and delving deep into your psyche.

Supermoon

Similar to the Blue Moon, the Supermoon carries with it additional energy for magickal amplification. A Supermoon is a time when the Full Moon or New Moon appears unusually near due to its position at the perigee—the closest point to Earth in its orbit.

ASIDE FROM SELECTING THE BEST MOON PHASE FOR YOUR RITUAL, YOU MAY ALSO WANT TO TIME IT WITH THE SIGN OR ELEMENT THAT RULES OVER YOUR INTENTION.

Lunar Eclipse

A Lunar Eclipse occurs when the Earth is positioned directly between the Moon and the Sun. Since it can only occur during a Full Moon, its effect on the night sky—and on our magick—is profound. It is important to avoid spell work during a lunar eclipse. Just as the light is eclipsed from the sky, the manifesting power of the Full Moon is eclipsed from the available energy. In fact, many feel that during a Lunar Eclipse, the Moon actually draws energy from us, not the other way around. Introspection, meditation, and rest are ideal activities during a Lunar Eclipse, followed by a replenishment ritual.

Lunar Eclipse Replenishment Ritual *To be used in replenishing energy following a Lunar Eclipse. Best performed when the Full Moon begins to wane.*

1 Cast a circle of light around a dark, quiet place. Lie in a supine position and close your eyes. Massage Moon water (see page 43) into your third eye, heart space, and belly, and place the crystal you used to charge the Moon water on your heart center. Breathe slowly, in and out, focusing on the growing warmth in the center of your chest.

2 Lie still until you feel your skin begin to buzz with energy. Visualize that as your heart beats, it sends lunar energy coursing through your bloodstream. Soak in the powerful vibrations and chant "I am replenished. I am energized" until the light radiates into your aura.

3 Release yourself from the ritual by gently rising, and carry the crystal with you until the New Moon to keep you energized during the waning period.

Other Timing Considerations: When timing your magick with the Moon, you may not want to wait for the best moon phase to perform your ritual. Luckily, there is an intuitive workaround: Simply alter the language of your intention. For example, perhaps you want to banish an addiction, but the Moon is currently in a waxing phase. Instead of waiting weeks for the waning phase, you could use the growing power of the Waxing Moon to increase your willpower. Or perhaps you would like to perform a money-drawing spell, but the Moon is currently waning. Instead of waiting for the waxing phase, you could use the decreasing power of the Waning Moon to lessen the amount of bills you receive.

Aside from selecting the best moon phase for your ritual, you may also want to time it with the sign or element that rules over your intention. For instance, if you want to perform a spell to increase your psychic ability, you would ideally choose a Waxing Moon in Cancer, the Water sign of intuition, emotion, and natural empathy. Because the Moon changes signs approximately every two to two and a half days, timing a phase with the zodiac can be a bit tricky, especially if you will be taking other astrological factors into account. As you will see, garnering extra energy from the Moon and the planets can be helpful but not absolutely necessary. For simple spells, aligning your magick with the phase of the Moon should be enough.

Ritual Moon Magick

The Moon has danced throughout history and folklore for as long as it has risen in the night sky, sometimes male, sometimes female, sometimes both, and still other times a genderless ball of bewitchment. In Western astrology and most modern witchcraft traditions, the Moon is associated with the feminine qualities bestowed upon it by the ancient Greeks, Egyptians, Native traditions, and countless other cultures throughout history.

Although ritual Moon magick need not take a gendered approach, you will notice that it often draws from the softer, inner you—that which is responsible for emotions, empathy, and how we perceive the world around us. In natural witchcraft, we refer to this is as our *inner lunar energy*, resonating from the Moon's ruling element of Water. Whether we are practicing solo or taking part in a Moon circle, this lunar energy is immeasurable in helping us attain magickal goals.

Moon Circles

Even if you are a solitary witch, power can sometimes be found in numbers. A Moon circle—a gathering of magickally minded folk who come together to honor the Moon's phase—can help you manifest a goal that requires an enormous level of energy you may not be capable of conjuring on your own. By combining your power and drawing down the energy of the Moon in unison, you can deepen the available well of magick for everyone involved. New Moon circles for setting intentions, Full Moon circles for manifesting or making room for abundance, or Dark Moon circles for shared introspection are all particularly powerful formations. In Wicca, these Full Moon circles are commonly known as *esbats*. A Moon circle can also be held to connect with the inner lunar energy that exists within all of us, which is sometimes referred to as a *Goddess circle*.

The Goddess and the Divine Feminine

In some neopagan religions, the Moon is used to invoke the Goddess, a personification of classical feminine energy: emotion, intuition, nurture, empathy, and compassion. Many Native traditions call upon this lunar energy from the Grandmother Moon, the emotional and intuitive counterpart to Mother Earth, while Wiccan traditions honor the Triple Goddess, the collective term given to the Maiden, Mother, and Crone. Each of these life stages is associated with an ancient Greek moon goddess and a moon phase. The *Maiden*, Artemis the Goddess of the Hunt, is the Waxing Moon. The *Mother*, Selene the Goddess of Fertility, is the Full Moon. And the *Crone*, Hecate the Goddess of the Underworld and Magick, is the Waning Moon. *Drawing down the Moon* in Goddess or Moon circles is a way of invoking each deity during their particular phase and soaking up their powerful lunar energy.

The "divine feminine" is a concept that recognizes the modern need to reconnect with and honor the female as a symbol of power in the world and is often associated with the fertile and nurturing energy of Gaia, the Mother Earth goddess.

In witchcraft, we use the divine feminine in a symbolic way to connect with our inner lunar energy. Although the concept seems exclusive to female-identified individuals, the energies of the divine feminine and the Goddess are accessible to all genders. The terms "female" and "male" merely refer to the yin/yang or passive/receptive energy that we all balance within ourselves. To take a non-gendered approach to ritual moon magick, you can use terms to fit your own experience, such as Inner Moon, Moon Circles, Triple Moon, or Sacred Moon.

Moontime, the name given to the time of menstruation by many Native traditions, is considered to be a sacred time, devoted to releasing old energy to make room for new, fertile energy. It has been observed that naturally occurring menstrual cycles are often synced with the Moon's waxing and waning, and the beginning of bleeding will typically occur on the Dark Moon. Whether or not menstruation is part of your life, the time surrounding the Dark Moon—the symbolic period of moontime—can be used to tap into your lunar energy.

CHAPTER 4

ELEMENTAL MAGICK

In Western astrology, there exist five elements of nature as defined by ancient alchemy. There are those that make up the physical world: Earth, Air, Fire, and Water. Then there is that element that escapes our senses. Also known as aether or quintessence, the Spirit element is the intangible substance of the otherworld. It fills the voids within our own material plane and comprises the human spirit and the sum of all that exists.

If you were to peel back the layers of natural witchcraft, at its very core you would find Spirit spinning its web around the four physical elements, holding them in perfect balance. *Retaining that balance* is a delicate business, one that recognizes the fact that an element is not merely the sum of its physical properties. Fire is not the just the flames that flicker from combustion, but the intensity that burns within. It is the drive behind both creativity and destruction, desire and passion. It is the warmth of the summer Sun, the spice of cayenne pepper, and the bright yellows and oranges of calendula petals. It is the purification of energy and a blazing path to change. Elements comprise the material world, but they also relate to the metaphysical one. They are the physical and spiritual manifestations of the energy in the universe and are the building blocks for all that exists. How we learn to balance the elements within ourselves and harness them in our practice is vital to empowering our magick.

Elements of Nature

Each element of nature is represented on the pentagram, the five-pointed star that in witchcraft symbolizes the entirety of the human spirit in balance. Some traditions believe that the elements are ordered here by proximity to Spirit—the perfected being—with Fire being closest, then Air, followed by Water, and finally Earth at the base. In natural witchcraft, however, we place equal value on all of the material elements, as we realize that we cannot access the Spirit element unless each is in balance.

Because Spirit rules over the four physical elements, it is represented at the top of the pentagram. This places Spirit in the seat of ascension and resonates fully with natural witchcraft as we strive to raise our energies above the material plane to reach into the etheric realm.

The four classical elements have an important place in astrology as well. Each is associated with planets, moon phases, and the zodiac signs in trine relationships (a soft aspect of 120 degrees apart) in what are known as *triplicities*. Cardinal directions, seasons, and other correspondences based on the Hermetic Order of the Golden Dawn, a nineteenth-century European magical order that has influenced much of Western occultism, are also considered when calling upon elemental magick.

SPIRIT

AIR

WATER

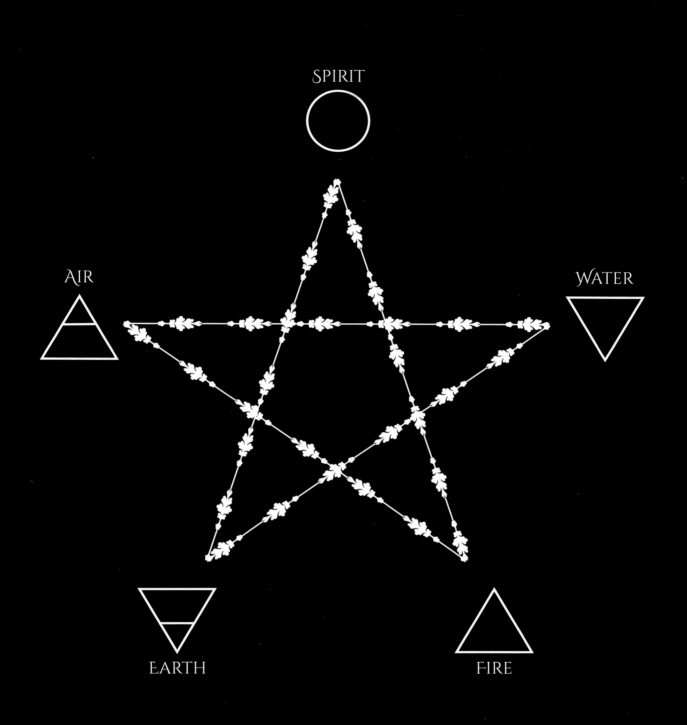

EARTH

FIRE

Balancing the Elements and Harnessing Their Power

Once mastered, elemental magick becomes quite intuitive. Upon integrating the elements into your practice, it will soon come naturally to you that Water is a sea of emotion associated with the Moon that pulls the tides, and that Earth is the stable ground we walk on, forever keeping us rooted. Like all aspects of nature, however, there are two sides to every element. Having too much or too little of any element in your astrological makeup can bring about a disharmony in yourself and your craft. In studying astrology, you will discover the planets and signs that exert the most influence over you, and your chart may reveal one or two elements with which you will experience a lifelong struggle.

For instance, too much Air in your chart can leave you up in the clouds without a tether to bring you back down to Earth, while too much Fire can set you ablaze with little to stop your path of destruction.

Balancing the elements, particularly when you are fighting an astrological imbalance, can seem daunting. But as natural witches, we are blessed with a strong connection to them. You will notice that the more time you spend in nature, the more intuitive this balance becomes (and the less likely you will be to need to focus on balancing them at all). Achieving this elemental equilibrium can bring about a personal growth that extends to your craft.

Harnessing the power of the elements alongside ritual work can evoke the Spirit element and draw down high vibrational energy. This is usually done by *calling the quarters*. There are also times in your practice when you may want to invite in the power of just a single element for magickal workings. For instance, if you were performing a spell to increase your wealth, you might want to call upon the Earth element, the element of material possessions and money. Each element can bring a unique energy to rituals or spells that enhance the nature of the work.

Calling the Quarters

In natural witchcraft, we seek not only to balance the elements within us but also to evoke the qualities of these forces of nature to add to our magickal practice. In especially powerful rituals, we can call upon the *four quarters*, or each cardinal direction that is associated with a physical element. By calling forth the raw power of each element, we can raise our energy to connect with the Spirit element and bring forth high-vibrational magick for our workings.

CALLING THE QUARTERS

To be performed before a ritual or spell that requires high-vibrational magick.

1 In calling the quarters, you must first determine where the cardinal direction of North is. North is associated with the Earth element and will be the first quarter that you evoke, as it is the physical matter with which we are most connected. Here you can place either a representation of the element or a candle in the correspondent color. Continue for each cardinal direction in a sunwise (deosil or clockwise) direction. For instance, you could place a bowl of soil or a green candle in the North for Earth, a feather or a yellow candle in the East for Air, a red candle or a smudge pot in the South for Fire, and a bowl of water or a blue candle in the West for Water. You may carve the alchemical symbols for the elements into each candle.

2 Calling the quarters can be as simple as meditating toward each direction, focusing on the individual energy that each element will bring to your magick as you light the candles. As you light each candle, focus on the individual energy that each element will bring to your magick and recite the following incantation to summon their qualities:

I call upon the North, the Element of Earth, bearer of strength and protection.

I call upon the East, the Element of Air, bearer of insight and wisdom.

I call upon the South, the Element of Fire, bearer of action and reaction.

I call upon the West, the Element of Water, bearer of intuition and emotion.

Then come back to the center and, in looking up, say: *"Spirit Element, bridge to ascension, I evoke thee."*

3 Now that you have the power of the elements in your circle, you can perform your chosen ritual or spell. When you are finished, you can release the elements in reverse order by thanking them and snuffing out the candles.

Fire △

Fire is the life force that rages in all of us. It is the drive, the passion, and the energy that ignites the spark of creation. Fire purifies through destruction and prepares the land for rebirth. It transforms, produces light and warmth, and cannot be grasped or contained.

SEASON	SUMMER
DIRECTION	SOUTH
TIME OF DAY	NOON
MOON PHASE	FULL MOON
QUALITIES	HOT AND DRY
ZODIAC SIGNS	SAGITTARIUS, ARIES, AND LEO
PLANETS	SUN, MARS, AND URANUS
TAROT SUIT	WANDS
COLORS	RED
TOOLS	WANDS AND RITUAL KNIVES
HERBS	CALENDULA, CINNAMON, NETTLE, ROSEMARY
CRYSTALS	AMBER, CARNELIAN, GARNET

Balancing Fire

There may be no other elemental imbalance as obvious as too much Fire. Fiery individuals often experience uncontrollable feelings of aggression and rage, an unstoppable desire for momentum, and a thirst for passion. They may crave attention in dangerous or inappropriate ways. An abundance of Fire in your chart can make relationships difficult, as the focus on activity and strength often overlooks the necessity for emotion and empathy. Intuition, too, is left behind, unable to escape the leaping flames.

Connecting with your inner, emotional self—that is, with Water—is a way to counter an abundance of Fire. Moon rituals, swimming, meditation, and even therapeutic crying or laughing sessions can be helpful in tapping into your emotional center. Finding ways to bring Water into your daily life, too, can help quench any sparks that might ignite if left unattended. A water feature such as a fountain, aquarium, or waterfall; ritual baths; rain soundtracks; drinking spring-fed water; or participation in water-based sports such as kayaking, fishing, or paddleboarding are all excellent ways to dampen the fire.

Fire Magick

Fire rules over passion, desire, strength, action, reaction, transformation, and purification. Rituals to ignite your inner flame, build confidence and assertiveness, imbue happiness and joy, as well as sex and love magick, are all greatly influenced by the element of Fire. In working with Fire magick, there is no source more powerful than the Sun itself, though candle spells and balefires can be used to harness the power of the flame as well. Solar magick, fire scrying, candle dressing and carving, ceremonial blade work, baking, and potion crafting over an open flame are all excellent ways to call forth the element of Fire.

PASSION CANDLE SPELL

❦

To be used for bringing passion or desire into your romantic life. Best performed while facing South under the Full Moon or the Noon Sun in Sagittarius, Aries, or Leo—a time under the Fire signs that kindles the cooling embers.

1 Sprinkle cinnamon on the twigs of a besom and symbolically cleanse a comfortable space by sweeping the negative energy out of an open door. Ensure that the besom does not physically touch the floor. This is a metaphysical cleansing only.

2 Dress a red pillar candle with a few drops of sweet almond oil and a pinch of cinnamon. As you rub the oil on the candle from wick to base with your fingertips, chant an intention like, "Ignite the desire within."

3 Light the candle and visualize that you are igniting the smoldering embers inside of you. As a small flame erupts, it spreads its warmth throughout your body.

4 Carefully dip your finger into the melted wax or pour a bit into your hand and massage it into your heart's center, continuing your chant.

5 Allow the candle to burn for as long as you can and relight it throughout the week in your presence until it has burned out completely.

Air △

As the Sun rises in the East, the direction of Air, it brings with it a new beginning. Air is the breath of life and the realm of intellect and insight. It is the element of communication—words are carried easily in the slightest breeze or howled into the wind. Air blows in, bringing the power of cleansing and the properties of the spirit into the physical realm. Without Air, there would be nothing: It breathes life into all of the other elements, just as ideas breathe life into creation.

SEASON	SPRING
DIRECTION	EAST
TIME OF DAY	SUNRISE
MOON PHASE	WAXING MOON
QUALITIES	HOT AND MOIST
ZODIAC SIGNS	GEMINI, LIBRA, AND AQUARIUS
PLANETS	VENUS AND JUPITER
TAROT SUIT	SWORDS
COLOR	YELLOW
TOOLS	FEATHERS, FANS, WOODWINDS
HERBS	EYEBRIGHT, LAVENDER, WORMWOOD
CRYSTALS	KYANITE, LAPIS LAZULI, AMETHYST

Balancing Air

An imbalance of Air affects the way in which we relate to our intellect. Too much Air can cause us to get lost in our ideas, our heads always in the clouds, dreaming of what could be. Airy individuals may sometimes find that they are described as all talk and no action. Philosophical waxing can be a powerful stimulant for growth, but if it is not brought down to reality and made concrete, it can become lost in the wind.

Balancing Air with the Earth element is a way to ground ourselves and develop a plan of action for our ideas. A routine that centers on the physical is a great way to set yourself up for success if you have a chart dominated by Air. A focus on diet and exercise as well as list writing and calendar keeping can help Airy individuals actively engage with their thoughts. Physical hobbies, too, can facilitate a connection with the Earth element. Gardening, chopping wood, hiking, rockhounding, pottery, and animal husbandry are all excellent activities for those looking to add a little Earth into their lives.

Air Magick

The elemental realm of Air rules over intelligence, communication, creativity, new beginnings, divination, and travel. Rituals to clear your mind, remove blockages, spark ideas, divine the future, or beckon opportunity are best performed under the influence of Air. Here, rituals should involve writing or speaking, as Air rules communication. Bells, wind chimes, and woodwind instruments like the flute or the recorder are also useful in evoking the Air element. Breathing exercises and meditation should also be considered. Hand fans and feathers can be used to move the air around and are particularly useful in fanning herbal or incense smoke.

Clearing the Mind *To be used for creative or writer's block, a blocked third eye, brain fog, or an inability to move forward in some aspect of your life. Best performed while facing East under the Waxing Moon in Gemini, Libra, or Aquarius—a time under the Air signs that brings with it cleansing, growth, and manifestation.*

1 Fan your sacred space with lavender smoke or spray using a hand fan or feather. Place a blank journal or art pad and a writing or painting implement such as a quill and ink or paintbrush on your desk or creative area. Call in the Air element by ringing a bell or playing a single repetitive note on a woodwind instrument.

2 Close your eyes. Pick up your writing or painting implement and, as you visualize the wind coming into your mind to sweep away cobwebs and clutter, begin to write or paint. Do so freely with big looping movements. Let the pen dance across the paper, flitting this way and that until your mind feels free and clear.

3 Open your eyes and look at your paper. Enjoy the movement that is visible in your lines, evidence that they have gone where the wind has taken them. Now, take a deep breath and then let it out slowly as you turn to a blank page to begin your work.

Water ▽

Water is a wave of emotion, sometimes gently fluxing and other times barrel-rolling its way through your life. Intuition, too, is guided by its ebb and flow. Your dreams and subconscious float lazily in its depths until you choose to dive deeply and explore that which lies beneath the surface. Empathy swells and psychic abilities expand as the element of Water shifts to fill any space it is in. It is healing and nurturing, and is the element that creates life.

SEASON	AUTUMN
DIRECTION	WEST
TIME OF DAY	DUSK
MOON PHASE	WANING MOON
QUALITIES	COLD AND MOIST
ZODIAC SIGN	CANCER, SCORPIO, AND PISCES
PLANETS	MOON, NEPTUNE
TAROT SUIT	CUPS
COLOR	BLUE
TOOLS	CHALICE, CAULDRON, SEASHELLS, AND RIVER STONES
HERBS	BURDOCK, ROSE, VALERIAN
CRYSTALS	OPAL, AQUAMARINE, MOONSTONE

Balancing Water

When a person's astrological chart is flooded with the Water element, they often find themselves swimming endlessly without ever reaching shore. They become trapped in their own whirlpool of emotions or list this way and that on a sailless boat. Passivity can overcome a watery person, resulting in a timid and a close-mouthed nature that appears complacent and naïve.

Fire can provide a beacon of light for a Watery person to swim to. It can light the embers of activity and reactivity as well as evaporate the excess of emotion you might be swimming in. Lighting candles and burning wood fires can connect you with the element of Fire. You might also invite in fiery correspondences like orange and yellow flowers, spicy cooking, adventurous exercise, therapeutic screaming, hot yoga, and kama sutra or other passion-bringing activities. Lighting your own fire can sometimes prove difficult, so you may want to combine forces with someone who helps ignite the spark, such as a close Fiery friend or lover.

Water Magick

The Water element influences emotion, empathy, psychic abilities, dreams, purification, and sleep. Rituals that are influenced by Water energy include moon magick, emotional healing, third-eye opening, lucid dreaming, and cleansing, as well as those for increasing friendship and bonding. To invite the Water element into your rituals, you may drink, anoint, or cleanse with elemental or Moon water or take a ritual bath or shower. Scrying in a black bowl filled with water or tea-leaf reading can enhance your divinatory practice. The Water element can also be harnessed by incorporating remnants of the sea such as conch shells or sea glass into your spellwork. Timing your work with the moon phases can bring additional Water energy to your rituals.

Recovering Lost Emotions *To be used for recovering emotions through lucid dreaming. Best performed while facing West under the Waning Moon in Cancer, Scorpio, or Pisces—a time under the Water signs that brings sleep and dreams.*

1 Energetically cleanse your bedroom with lavender and mugwort smoke or spray (see page 31). Place a piece of amethyst under your pillow, and lie down. Lightly massage mugwort and lavender-infused coconut oil or a *dream salve* (see Flying Ointment on page 138) into your third eye. Lightly spray a sleep mask or small pillow with lavender water, or fill a small sachet with lavender and mugwort. Close your eyes and place the mask or pillow over your eyes.

2 Focus on the emotion with which you want to connect. As your body begins to relax, make a conscious effort to remain present. Visualize the emotion glowing in front of you, so close you can almost grasp it. But it soars away, and you start after it. Feel your breath leave and enter your body as you run after it, crossing a seemingly never-ending expanse of beach. A salty sea finally emerges from the sand and in the distance a beacon of light blinks through the fog. You enter the sea and swim toward the light until you reach a lighthouse perched above a craggy rock. Making your way up the crumbling spiral steps until you finally reach the top, you spot a door. You open the door and inside is the beacon—your glowing emotion. Remove it from its platform and wear it around your neck like a necklace as you row a dinghy back to the physical realm.

3 When you return from your lucid state, visualize that this emotional jewel is now a part of your metaphysical wardrobe.

Earth ▽

As solid as the ground we stand on, Earth is the physical matter that we can grasp in our hands. It is our body rooted in pragmatism and practicality. Earth is the base of all elements and relates to more than just the rocks and soil of the material world. Money, career, possessions, diet, and physical care—all of these are Earthly matters.

SEASON	WINTER
DIRECTION	NORTH
TIME OF DAY	MIDNIGHT
MOON PHASE	NEW MOON
QUALITIES	COLD AND DRY
ZODIAC SIGNS	CAPRICORN, TAURUS, AND VIRGO
PLANETS	MERCURY AND SATURN
TAROT SUIT	PENTACLES
COLOR	GREEN
TOOLS	SOIL, ROCKS, AND SALT
HERBS	OAK, SAGE, VETIVER
CRYSTALS	BLACK TOURMALINE, GREEN AVENTURINE, JADE

Balancing Earth

An abundance of Earth in our charts can leave us too rooted in the ground. We may seem overly pessimistic, rigid, stubborn, and apathetic, and we might be labeled as perfectionists. Logic and practicality can drag down any hopes or dreams that may float among the clouds.

Inviting Air into your life can shake things up and loosen the packed-down soil. Dancing, yoga, acting, dream work, philosophical discussions, and long walks are great additions to an Earthy person's routine. Really, anything that is relaxing, uplifting, or freeing can counterbalance an abundance of the Earth element. Simple, everyday things, too, like opening the windows, hanging windchimes and weathervanes, bird-watching, and butterfly gardening can allow air to flow through your life. Of course, if you are feeling adventurous, you can always go skydiving or hang gliding!

Earth Magick

The elemental realm of Earth rules over stability, protection, wealth, career, physical health, the home, and nature. Earth rituals should include physical remnants of nature, such as rocks or crystals, soil, plants, iron or metal ore, and wood or twigs. Rituals could include something as simple as setting out a bowl of soil or salt on your altar, or they could focus on weaving Earth magick into more complex crafts like knot magick, blacksmithing, wood or stone carving, or crafting brick dust or other protection powders. Grounding rituals are particularly powerful under the element of Earth.

Grounding Ritual *To be used for finding focus in preparation for setting goals or intentions. Best performed while facing North under the New Moon in Capricorn, Taurus, or Virgo—a time under the Earth signs that brings centeredness.*

1 Find a cool, shady spot where you are in direct contact with the soil. (Alternatively, bring a bowl of soil to your sacred space and set all of your plants around you.) Lightly bury a piece of hematite or black tourmaline (grounding stones) in the soil. Energetically cleanse the space with sage, cedar smoke, or spray.

2 Close your eyes and beat a drum slowly and repetitively until you can feel the echo of it beat into the Earth. Continue the beat until the Earth responds. Feel the soil begin to vibrate as you beat; watch as the trees or plants respond to the reverberations. Feel the reverberations enter your throat and your chest as your drumbeat and the pulse of the Earth become one. Visualize that the roots of the trees and plants pulsate with each beat of your heart as you continue to beat on the drum in time with your pulse. When you feel that you and the Earth have become one, slowly taper off the beating of the drum until it is barely audible.

3 Dig up the hematite or black tourmaline and carry it with you whenever you are in need of grounding.

Spirit ○

Spirit is the universal energy that we call upon to empower our spells, inform our divinatory practice, and ascend to the etheric plane. It is both nothing and everything. It takes up no space, yet it fills completely. In traditional Indian cosmology, it is called *Akasha*, a term that was brought into Western occultism through the Theosophy movement.

In natural witchcraft, we refer to it as aether, quintessence, or the universal life force. The knowledge that the Spirit element contains is boundless, for within its finely woven fabric is the entirety of the human experience—past, present, and future. It is the aether that gave birth to the four physical elements and it is the *dark energy* or *dark matter* that is responsible for the expanding universe. In the body, the Spirit element is associated with the third eye and can be accessed through meditation, divination, energy elevation, and the release of the etheric body from the physical body.

DIRECTION	**EVERYWHERE**
TIME OF DAY	**ETERNAL**
MOON PHASE	**DARK OR FULL MOON**
COLORS	**BLACK, WHITE, OR VIOLET**
TOOL	**DIVINATION**

Spirit is always present in high-vibrational magick and thus requires no specific ritual for general spellwork. Your own expanded energy is all that is required to meet it. Specific rituals to access the Spirit element in divination and spirit communication will be described in Chapter 9.

OUROBOROS

The ouroboros, the mysterious symbol depicting a serpent or dragon eating its own tail, first appeared in the ancient Egyptian text engraved on the Enigmatic Book of the Netherworld, the second gilded shrine of King Tutankhamun. There, it symbolized the cyclical journey of the Sun. In alchemy, the ouroboros is associated with the philosopher's stone and thus with immortality. Norse mythology claimed the ouroboros, too, envisioning it as a child of Loki and Angrboða that could grow so large it could wrap itself around the world and bite its own tail. In Greek, *ouroboros* means "tail devourer" and is sometimes depicted as a figure eight in the symbol of infinity. Victorians honored the ouroboros as a symbol of resurrection: It appeared on tombstones in their cemeteries and in their mourning jewelry, where it represented an eternal bond with the deceased. In modern-day witchcraft, we use the ouroboros as a symbol for rebirth after we acknowledge and integrate the shadow self. Self-destruction is needed for growth, and it is through the ouroboros—the devouring of our old selves—that we achieve a higher state of being. Through death, there is life.

CHAPTER 5

ASTROLOGY

Western astrology is a system based on thousands of years of celestial observation, which we humans have used both to define ourselves and to divine aspects of our lives and the world around us. In keeping with nature-based witchcraft, we understand that just as we are but tiny creatures in a vast world, ours is but a tiny world in a vast universe. When you are born, the astronomical bodies are arranged in such a way as to reveal your unique impression on the world.

As you go through life, these objects travel from their positions in your birth sky and transit through the constellations on their unique ecliptic paths. Their relative positions to those on your birth chart or *natal chart*—a snapshot of the sky at the time of your birth—affect every facet of your being, including your magick. A deep dive into your birth chart can help you to understand what makes you and your magick tick and to align it with the cosmos.

The Zodiac: Astrological Houses, Signs, and Planets

The basis for all astrological movements in the sky is a belt of constellations known as the zodiac. Over the course of a year (the time it takes for Earth to orbit the Sun), these twelve constellations appear to slowly spin around us. They expand through each of the astrological houses dividing our birth sky, leaving indelible marks on the areas of our lives that they touch. The planets follow their own ecliptic paths, forming aspects with one another as they transit through the zodiac. Understanding how the celestial bodies form these relationships in the context of astrological houses and signs, and then applying that knowledge to our birth charts, can bring a sense of strength and attunement to our practice.

Houses

The twelve houses that make up the astrological sky on our birth chart are arranged in a wheel similar to that of the zodiac. The wheel of houses, however, is fixed to our chart. Each of the houses relates to an area of human experience, beginning at the self and traveling outward to society and then beyond, to the realm of mysticism. It is in these areas of our lives that the signs and planets express themselves, whether on your natal chart (at birth) or by transit (current). While each sign and planet has a "home," or is said to "live" in a particular house (and each sign and planet will best manifest its energy in the house in which it "lives"), they are all in a constant state of motion. As they travel through the houses, they bring their unique energy to different areas of your life.

PLANETS
⊙ SUN
☽ MOON
☿ MERCURY
♀ VENUS
♂ MARS
♃ JUPITER
♄ SATURN
♅ URANUS
♆ NEPTUNE
♇ PLUTO

SIGNS
♈ ARIES
♉ TAURUS
♊ GEMINI
♋ CANCER
♌ LEO
♍ VIRGO
♎ LIBRA
♏ SCORPIO
♐ SAGITTARIUS
♑ CAPRICORN
♒ AQUARIUS
♓ PISCES

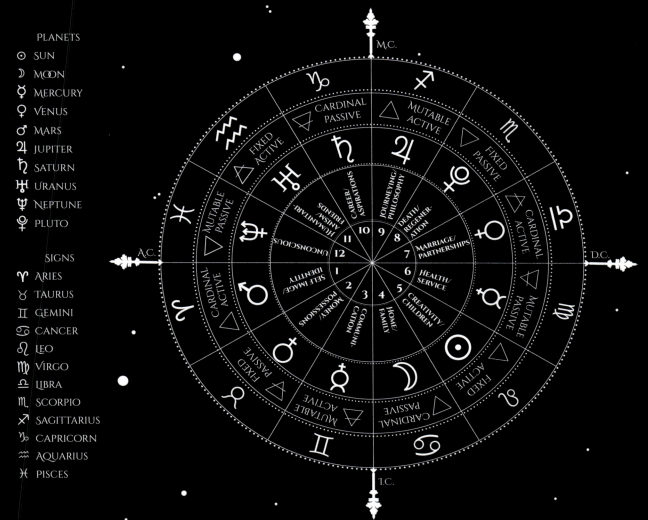

Signs and Their Traits

Sun Sign: As the Earth orbits the Sun, the Sun appears to pass through each of the zodiac constellations month by month, giving rise to what we know as the astrological Sun Signs. In ancient times, stargazers observed that those born under the same constellation shared core personality traits based on corresponding elements, qualities, polarities, and ruling planets. Although there are many facets to "your sign," the Sun is the brightest part of your personality—the very essence of *you*.

Moon Sign

Just as the Sun passes through each of the constellations of the zodiac, so does the Moon. And just as you were born with the Sun in a certain zodiac sign, you were born with the Moon in a certain zodiac sign. However, while your Sun Sign reflects the you that shines, your Moon Sign reveals the part of you that is hidden away from others. The Moon is ruled by the element of Water and governs your emotions and your inner self.

Rising Sign

As you arrived Earthside, a zodiac constellation was rising above the horizon in the East in the first astrological house on your birth chart. This constellation is your Rising Sign or Ascendant, and it is your first impression, or the outer "you" that you present to the world. Your Rising Sign determines the order in which the zodiac signs will occupy your houses, and you will need your exact time of birth to calculate it.

There are three characteristics to consider when looking at zodiac signs, which, along with their ruling planets, can help you determine their traits without memorizing them. These characteristics are element, quality, and polarity.

Elements

The constellations of the zodiac are grouped together by their association with each of the four physical elements: Fire (Aries, Leo, and Sagittarius); Earth (Taurus, Virgo, and Capricorn); Air (Gemini, Libra, and Aquarius); and Water (Cancer, Scorpio, and Pisces). Each element bestows its unique qualities on the signs with which it is associated. Air brings intellect and sociability. Fire brings passion and drive. Water brings emotion and fluidity. Earth brings density and materialism.

Qualities

Qualities (or modalities) in astrology can be thought of as the way (or mode) in which a sign will express the needs of its element. There are three qualities of an element: Cardinal, Fixed, and Mutable. Cardinal signs start things. They are ambitious, blazing their own paths through the world. Each cardinal sign is associated with an equinox or solstice and begins a new season. Fixed signs, on the other hand, are steady and systematic. They like to stabilize. Mutable signs come at the end of a season. They are always changing. They adapt to any situation and will often look for creative ways to finish projects that

CAPRICORN
RESPONSIBLE
AUTHORITATIVE
AMBITIOUS

SAGITTARIUS
OPTIMISTIC
PHILOSOPHICAL
INDEPENDENT

AQUARIUS
ECCENTRIC
INTELLECTUAL
UNPREDICTABLE

SCORPIO
INTUITIVE
FOCUSED
SECRETIVE

PISCES
ARTISTIC
SENSITIVE
EMPATHETIC

LIBRA
BALANCED
CHARMING
INDECISIVE

ARIES
ENERGETIC
ASSERTIVE
FEARLESS

VIRGO
PERFECTIONISTIC
PRACTICAL
ANALYTICAL

TAURUS
RELIABLE
SENSUAL
CAUTIOUS

LEO
CHARISMATIC
EXPRESSIVE
DRIVEN

GEMINI
COMMUNICATIVE
CURIOUS
ADAPTIVE

CANCER
CREATIVE
EMPATHETIC
SPONTANEOUS

DEC 22-
JAN 19

NOV 22-
DEC 21

JAN 20-
FEB 18

OCT 23-
NOV 21

FEB 19-
MAR 20

SEP 23-
OCT 22

MAR 21-
APR 19

AUG 23-
SEP 22

APR 20-
MAY 20

JUL 23-
AUG 22

MAY 21-
JUN 20

JUN 21-
JUL 22

the cardinal sign began and the fixed sign worked steadily on. Not coincidentally, those born under mutable signs may not always align with the traits of their zodiac.

Now we can place elemental traits within the context of their qualities for each Sun Sign. If a person's Sun Sign is in Aries, for instance, they have the cardinal quality of Fire, and thus they have the habit of starting new things with an unparalleled fervor before quickly moving on. Someone born under the fixed Earth sign, Taurus, however, exhibits a very grounded, stable nature, approaching things with pragmatism and consistency. The mutable Air sign, Gemini, rides the breeze of insight, collecting information as they go and adapting their decisions to their ever-increasing breadth of knowledge.

Polarities

When horoscopes speak of zodiac sign compatibility, they base this compatibility on polarities. Polarity, often referred to as feminine/masculine or yin/yang, can also be thought of as positive/negative, or, in modern astrology, active/passive. Active signs are more assertive while passive signs are more receptive. Fire and Air signs are active (energetic) while Earth and Water signs are receptive (calm). You can think of the compatibility between these seemingly oppositional signs in this way: Air feeds Fire and Water sustains Earth. This natural affinity for balance is the basis for the astrological phenomenon of "opposites attract." On the zodiac wheel, you can find six pairs of polar signs, or *astrological mirrors*, which are directly across from each other at 180 degrees.

T HERE ARE THREE CHARACTERISTICS TO CONSIDER WHEN LOOKING AT ZODIAC SIGNS. THESE CHARACTERISTICS ARE ELEMENT, QUALITY, AND POLARITY.

Planets

In astrology, the term "planets" is not limited to the planets that appear in the traditional solar system: it also encompasses the Sun, Moon, and even asteroids. (The Sun and Moon are often referred to as *luminaries*.) As the planets travel through the houses and the zodiac wheel on our chart, they alter the way that we perceive and interact with the different areas of our lives.

There are a number of ways that planets can influence us, from the overarching effect of the ruling planet of our chart determined by our Rising Sign, to the energy of the planets that traveled our houses at birth, to the planets actively transiting today's sky. In this section, we will take a brief look at the ruling planets for the zodiac signs, then address planetary chart rulers and transits, an aspect made between the current position of a planet to the planets on your natal chart later on (see page 79). An aspect made between the current position of a planet to the planets on your natal chart is called a transit.

Ruling Planets

Each natal planet has an effect on our astrological makeup. However, it is the ruling planet that exerts the most influence over a given zodiac sign. A ruling planet can be thought of as the planet that makes its home or domicile in a particular zodiac sign. Because Uranus, Neptune, and Pluto were not discovered until the invention of telescopes, modern astrologers have amended the ancient ruling planets to include them. This is why you will see Scorpio, Aquarius, and Pisces with secondary ruling planets. These co-rulerships exhibit dual traits that work together based on their modern and ancient rulers.

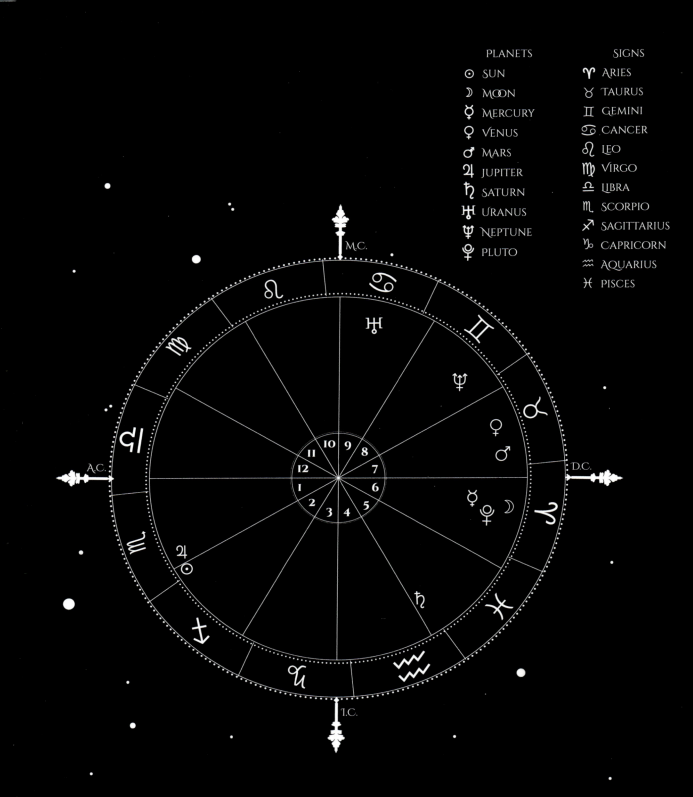

PLANETS

- ☉ SUN
- ☽ MOON
- ☿ MERCURY
- ♀ VENUS
- ♂ MARS
- ♃ JUPITER
- ♄ SATURN
- ♅ URANUS
- ♆ NEPTUNE
- ♇ PLUTO

SIGNS

- ♈ ARIES
- ♉ TAURUS
- ♊ GEMINI
- ♋ CANCER
- ♌ LEO
- ♍ VIRGO
- ♎ LIBRA
- ♏ SCORPIO
- ♐ SAGITTARIUS
- ♑ CAPRICORN
- ♒ AQUARIUS
- ♓ PISCES

Understanding Natal Charts

Astrological Houses: Your birth chart is a snapshot of the sky at the moment of your birth. The wheel of houses acts as its framework and is the same for each person's chart. The zodiac wheel spins around this framework of houses so that the sign that was rising in the East at the time of your birth is on the cusp of the first house. This point, the *Ascendant*, will always appear at the leftmost part of the chart.

Directly across from the Ascendant is the sign that was setting on the western horizon. This is known as the *Descendant*. Moving in a counterclockwise motion, you can trace the houses around from the Ascendant to catch a glimpse of how the planets and signs were aligned in the different areas of your life at birth. The first six houses reveal what was hidden below the horizon at the moment of your birth and represent the *personal* areas of your life. The last six houses show what was above the horizon in the visible sky and thus represent the *interpersonal* areas of your life. Although all of the astrological houses are vital to achieving a complete picture of your life experience, we will focus on the Angular or *Cardinal* houses—those houses whose angles make up the cusps of the four houses that will have the greatest impact on you—the Ascendant (A.C.), Descendant (D.C.), Midheaven (M.C.), and *Imum Coeli* (I.C.). Exploring these houses on your chart will give you insight into how you approach the four cornerstones of your life: self, home, relationships, and goals.

Signs

The Ascendant or Rising Sign (e.g. Libra Rising) is always the cusp of the first house. Your Rising Sign reveals how others perceive you: your appearance, demeanor, and the kind of first impression you make. Think of it like this: If your Sun Sign were to write a monologue, your Rising Sign would be the actor delivering it. Your Rising Sign also reveals your planetary chart ruler and gives you an idea of what the central theme in your life will be. For example, if your Rising Sign were Libra, then your planetary chart ruler would be Venus. Having Venus as a chart ruler would place an emphasis on beauty, harmony, wealth, and materialism, and finding where your planetary chart ruler was transiting on your birth chart could give you further insight into how you approach these aspects of your life. To complete the above example, if your Rising Sign, Libra, and your planetary chart ruler, Venus, were transiting the Seventh House—the house of Relationships—in fiery Aries, you might thrive on the idea of being part of an exciting and dynamic couple, and may strive for balance via passionate arguments, competition, and spontaneity. It is worth noting here that the transits (or real time position) of your planetary chart ruler will be more important than any other transits throughout your life.

Once you have established your Rising Sign and your planetary chart ruler, you can then locate the Sun and Moon on your chart and determine how each of them manifests within its sign and how each lights up the astrological houses it is in.

For instance, if your Sun were in passionate and possessive Scorpio in the second house, the house of wealth, you might believe that having money brings you power and emotional security. A struggle to balance your finances may make you intensely possessive over material objects, particularly if your Moon were also in the second house, encouraging emotional attachment.

Planets

After determining your birth chart signs, you can locate the planets on your chart and note the relationships that they form with each other, paying close attention to the Cardinal Houses. The inner planets—the Sun, Moon, Mercury, Venus, and Mars—are considered the personal planets, and reflect the way in which we express ourselves. The outer planets—Jupiter, Saturn, Uranus, Neptune, and Pluto—are the unseen depths of our selves. As we travel from the inner planets to the outer planets, their influence on our chart becomes less immediately apparent.

Aspects

The relationships that planets form with each other due to time and distance are known as *aspects*. In astrology, there are major and minor aspects, depending on the distance and level of influence the relationship brings to your chart. For the purposes of this book, we will consider only five of the major aspects. Trines and Sextiles are *soft aspects*, which are easy and harmonious relationships between planets. Oppositions and Squares are *hard aspects*, which are tense and difficult. Conjunctions are *neutral aspects* and can go either way.

CONJUNCTION: Neutral. Planets that are in conjunction in your chart are planets that are 0 degrees apart (with a 6-degree margin) and appear to move together in the same sign. This can be either harmonious or not, depending on whether the characteristics of the planets are compatible.

TRINE: Soft. Planets that are four signs apart (120 degrees) have the same ruling element and speak of something that will come naturally to you throughout your life.

SEXTILE: Soft. Planets that are 60 degrees apart are said to be sextile and can cooperate with ease. The areas of life in which they communicate will be characterized by a sense of comfort and familiarity.

OPPOSITION: Hard. Planets that are across from each other (or 180 degrees apart) are said to be in polarity or in opposition. This is a hard aspect, since the planets are in a state of tension and can be thought of as irreconcilable forces. Finding a balance between each planet's perceived weakness is the key to overcoming oppositions and cultivating a complementary relationship.

SQUARE: Hard. Planets that are 90 degrees apart are said to be square of each other, and each will pull in its own direction. The need for these planets to reconcile and compromise will make decisions involving the two difficult or challenging.

RITUAL FOR HONORING YOUR PLANETARY CHART RULER

To be used for honoring your planetary chart ruler. Best performed on the day and time ruled by your planetary chart ruler.

1 Determine the element of your planetary chart ruler, and choose twelve candles in a color representative of that element: Earth (green), Air (yellow), Fire (red), or Water (blue). Carve the symbol of your planetary chart ruler into each candle as a way to honor its influence on each of your astrological houses.

2 Place the candles in a circle around you and, beginning with the candle at the easternmost point of the circle, light each candle around the wheel of houses in a counterclockwise direction. At each candle's house, note how your planetary chart ruler influences this area of your life. At the candle of the first house, you might say, "Thank you, Venus, for bringing beauty, charm, style, and charisma to my outer Self."

3 Once you have finished lighting the candles, sit facing the current transiting point of your planetary chart ruler and bathe in its energy. During this time, you could consider the overarching effect your planetary chart ruler has on your life. For instance, Jupiter influences growth and prosperity.

4 End your ritual by giving thanks to its special influence on your life. For instance, for an Aquarius Rising with a planetary chart ruler of Uranus, you could say, "I honor the originality and uniqueness I present to the world."

5 Allow the candles to burn out completely or extinguish them one by one, moving in a counterclockwise direction.

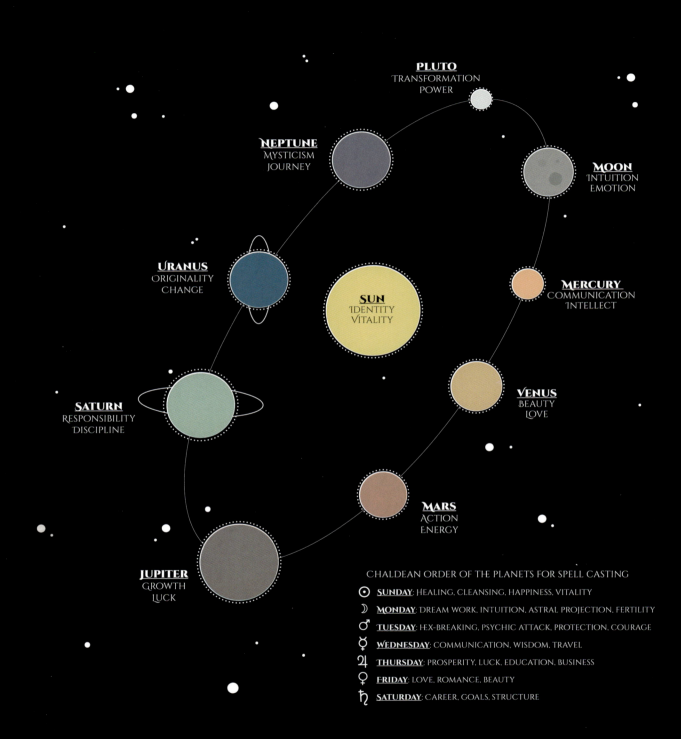

PLUTO
TRANSFORMATION
POWER

NEPTUNE
MYSTICISM
JOURNEY

MOON
INTUITION
EMOTION

URANUS
ORIGINALITY
CHANGE

SUN
IDENTITY
VITALITY

MERCURY
COMMUNICATION
INTELLECT

SATURN
RESPONSIBILITY
DISCIPLINE

VENUS
BEAUTY
LOVE

MARS
ACTION
ENERGY

JUPITER
GROWTH
LUCK

CHALDEAN ORDER OF THE PLANETS FOR SPELL CASTING

☉ **SUNDAY**: HEALING, CLEANSING, HAPPINESS, VITALITY

☽ **MONDAY**: DREAM WORK, INTUITION, ASTRAL PROJECTION, FERTILITY

♂ **TUESDAY**: HEX-BREAKING, PSYCHIC ATTACK, PROTECTION, COURAGE

☿ **WEDNESDAY**: COMMUNICATION, WISDOM, TRAVEL

♃ **THURSDAY**: PROSPERITY, LUCK, EDUCATION, BUSINESS

♀ **FRIDAY**: LOVE, ROMANCE, BEAUTY

♄ **SATURDAY**: CAREER, GOALS, STRUCTURE

When the Planets Align: How Planets Affect Your Magick

Ancient astrologers observed that the planets had profound effects on Earthly life as they traveled at various speeds through the zodiac. Aside from their influence on our natal charts, the planets can affect our day-to-day lives or can even span entire generations. The planets that are closer to the Sun have smaller orbits and thus travel through the zodiac more quickly than planets with larger orbits.

For instance, Mercury, the closest planet to the Sun, has an orbital period of 88 days. Pluto, on the other hand, takes an astounding 248 years to make its way around our star. This means that while Mercury will travel through each zodiac sign within the space of a year, it will take Pluto 14 to 30 years just to move from one sign to the next.

Astrologers look to these transit times to determine what sort of impact the planets will have on our lives. The shorter the transit time, the more quickly a planet will cycle through the zodiac, and the more influential it will be in our daily lives. Conversely, the longer the transit time, the greater the chance that the planet's transit will exert an influence over your entire lifespan (or even the lifespans of your children). For this reason, the outer planets such as Uranus, Neptune, and Pluto are considered to have a *generational influence* on society.

In addition to transiting through zodiac signs, planets also exhibit changing relationships with each other over our lifespans. Although you can certainly look at current aspects of planets in the sky to make worldly predictions, observing them in relation to your natal chart can help you understand how they affect you and your magick most significantly in the present. An aspect made between the current position of a planet to the planets on your natal chart is called a transit. In preparing for your rituals, you should ensure that there are no hard aspects to the ruling planet of your spell in your chart that may decrease the amount of available energy from the planet.

Planetary Alignment for Magick Making

Each spell or ritual in your practice will fall under the influence of one or more planets, and timing your work with their transits can energize your magick beyond the Moon and the elements. Although there are many nuances to planetary alignment, using the day of the week as well as the Moon Sign is all that is necessary for most spells.

A simple example is a good fortune spell, which would be most strongly influenced by lucky Jupiter. Knowing that Jupiter has a lengthy orbit, however, and that it would be nearly impossible to wait until it is at home in Sagittarius, we could instead align our magick with Jupiter's day of the week—Thursday—and a Jupiter-influenced moon. A Waxing Moon—the moon phase of growth and expansion—in Jupiter's domicile of Sagittarius would be ideal in this case.

PLANETARY RETRO-GRADES

Mentioning the phrase "Mercury Retrograde" can strike fear into the heart of many witches. But, like most everything in astrology, planetary retrogrades are just another way for us to align our magick with the cosmos. Retrogrades occur when Earth passes a planet in orbit and the planet then appears to spin backward. During this time, it is best to avoid actions or spells that might fall under the influence of the retrograde planet. Instead center your magick on words that start with "re:" *reviewing, reworking, reimagining,* and *restoring.* Once the planet has gone direct (that is, the Earth has completed its orbit around it, and the planet no longer appears to spin backward), take action on all that you planned during the retrograde period. For example, during Mercury Retrograde, communication may go haywire. During this time, it is best to avoid having important conversations, sending hastily written emails or texts, or performing networking spells. Instead spend this time in introspection: Write in your journal, brush up on your knowledge, or communicate your own needs to yourself. In this way, although you are not actively performing spellwork, you are still aligning your magick with the planets.

The Chaldean Sequence

If your spell or ritual cannot be put on hold until the proper planetary alignment is in place but you would still like to call upon the energies of particular planets, there is a method by which you can use the hours of the day to bring luminary magick to your craft. The Chaldean Order of the Planets, which is based on the planetary spheres model and ordered from farthest (slowest moving) to nearest (fastest moving), is the framework you can use to calculate the hours of the day during which you can best draw these planetary energies. Although modern astrology considers planetary hour magick to be elective, ancient alchemy and herbalism consider it to be an indispensable tool. While you can certainly dig into the mathematics for calculating the planetary hours based on the sunrise in your location, a planetary hours calculator is available on astrology.com.tr/ planetary-hours.asp.

CHAPTER 6

∝✧๑

SEASONAL MAGICK

As the winds shift, so do the seasons of the witch. When the squalls blow hard and swift, our craft turns to the home and hearth, and when the leaves litter the ground, the time to call upon the spirits is approaching. The seasons comprise all of what we have learned thus far—the elements, moon magick, and astrology—but they also incorporate several things we have mentioned only in passing, such as the seasonal full moons and the ancient pagan celebrations that accompany solar magick.

Although modern witchcraft generally focuses on the power of the Moon, solar magick honors the heavenly body that is most vital to us here on Earth.

As we orbit the Sun on our axis, the intensity of its rays waxes and wanes throughout the year, bringing great changes to nature and to our magickal relationship with it. Meteorology recognizes just four seasons, but many of the world's regions tune into their own rhythms of nature and hold to a more nuanced calendar. For instance, there is monsoon season in some parts of East Asia, and wildfire season in the western United States and Australia. So, although we will be focusing on the eight seasonal celebrations called for by the neopagan Wheel of the Year as well as the seasonal Full Moons in this chapter, it is good to become acquainted with the seasonal nuances in your region and to honor them in their own right.

Seasonal Full Moons

Long before it was understood that the passing of the Sun could mark time and distinguish the seasons, ancient civilizations marked their calendars by the Moon. When the Moon began to rise earlier and set later, the soil hardened and the crops withered. And when it retreated in favor of the Sun, the snow and ice melted, giving way to fertile land. Each Full Moon illuminated the fields throughout the night, watching the last crops being harvested or the wolves howling in hunger among the trees.

In modern witchcraft, these Full Moons are often celebrated alongside the Wheel of the Year, and during these times we can reflect on what lies before us in the month ahead and how we can tune in with our magick. Modern pagan correspondences and names of the seasonal Full Moons originate from observations by Native American tribes, Anglo-Saxons, Celtics, Europeans, Colonial Americans, and Wiccans and vary by geographical region. The names that follow were widely used across Europe in the late eighteenth century, and additional names from other cultures and regions are included. Again, the names for the seasonal Full Moons that you choose to use should correspond to your own regional observations or cultural heritage. For example, the Algonquin names resonate with me because I live in the native Algonquian region of New England, and their land is what I connect with most. Depending on your own observations, you may even choose to rename the Full Moons entirely.

January: *Hunger Moon* (*Wolf Moon, Cold Moon, Old Moon, Moon After Yule, Snow Moon, Winter Moon, Ice Moon*)

It is here, in the most frigid month of the year, that you hear the wolves howl. They are hungry, circling the forest and plains, searching the barren land for their next meal. What does the wolf have to teach us about hunger? Without its pack, a wolf is left to hunt alone in the cold. Our family is what keeps us from starving, both physically and magickally. The Hunger Moon, then, is a reminder that we cannot rely only on ourselves. Honoring the connections we share with loved ones can feed us on every level. Rituals to perform during the January Full Moon could include kitchen magick and baking spells for bonding and protection spells for the home and family.

February: *Snow Moon* (*Quickening Moon, Hunger Moon, Opening Buds Moon, Trapper's Moon*)

The snow falls steadily and heavily in the month of February in many regions in the northern hemisphere. The log pile is dwindling, the root cellar nearly empty; but the call of Spring is near. The days are getting longer, and now we begin to plan for the busy months ahead. We order seeds, mentally plotting gardens and fields, and feel the flurry of activity in our minds and spirits begin to pick up. Rituals to perform during the February

JANUARY	FEBRUARY	MARCH
HUNGER MOON	**SNOW MOON**	**WORM MOON**

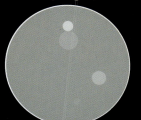  

APRIL	MAY	JUNE
PINK MOON	**FLOWER MOON**	**ROSE MOON**

  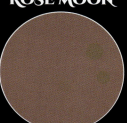

JULY	AUGUST	SEPTEMBER
BUCK MOON	**STURGEON MOON**	**CORN MOON**

 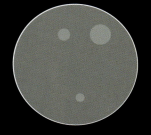 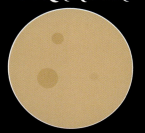

OCTOBER	NOVEMBER	DECEMBER
HUNTER MOON	**BEAVER MOON**	**COLD MOON**

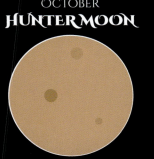 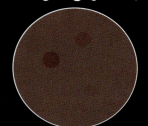 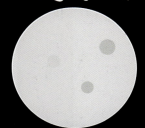

Full Moon could include purging addictions or bad habits that we may have picked up over the winter or ancestral work to help uncover our intentions for the months to follow.

March: *Worm Moon* (*Sap Moon, Crow Moon, Storm Moon, Crust Moon, Lenten Moon*)

In March, the worms begin to surface, calling the robins to come pluck them from the freshly tilled garden soil. The cawing of the crows sounds off across the land, signaling an end to winter. Here in Maine, sap flows freely from tapped Maple trees as the freezing nights give way to sundrenched days. During this transitional time between Winter and Spring, seeds are carefully nurtured in preparation for planting. Rituals to perform during the March Full Moon could include planting seeds or setting intentions, awakening energy spells, and cleansing rituals for the home and aura.

April: *Pink Moon* (*Rain Moon, Wind Moon, Sprouting Grass Moon, Egg Moon, Fish Moon, Frog Moon*)

Spring has officially arrived in many parts of the world by now, and pink phlox begins to carpet the land. This early sign of Spring in North America brings with it fertility, blossoming, and health. Nests are woven and filled with eggs, and rain showers drench the thirsty seedlings in the fields. The frogs croak and the fish spawn, and all the land seems to brim with the promise of new life. Rituals for the April Full Moon could include romance, love, and fertility spells, healing spells, creativity spells, or prosperity spells.

May: *Flower Moon* (*Corn Planting Moon, Milk Moon, Budding Moon*)

What were once bulbs buried deep in the frozen soil now become beautiful flowers that spring forth in an array of colors. Fruit trees blossom, peonies bloom, and violets upon violets blanket the pastures. The bees buzz from flower to flower and all the land is busy and bursting with life. Rituals for the May Full Moon could include beauty spells and enchantments, flower essence crafting, faerie magick, and productivity rituals.

June: *Rose Moon* (*Sun Moon, Strawberry Moon, Strong Moon, Hot Moon*)

The fruits of our labor are ripe for picking under June's Full Moon. Rose gardens are in full bloom, juicy strawberries line the paths, and the Sun heats the land as nature bestows its sweet bounty on us all. Rituals for the June Full Moon could include abundance spells, taking stock of and refining your goals, and celebrating all that nature has provided.

July: *Buck Moon* (*Thunder Moon, Hay Moon, Deer Moon, Blessing Moon*)

Deer and moose bucks grow their first antlers during this stormy, mid-summer month. Nature has provided for them, and they are growing into happy, thriving animals that traverse the tasty forest seeking the cool waters of streams and rivers. This is a powerful moon, full of strength and brawn. Electricity fills the skies, and we truly feel like we can accomplish anything. Rituals for the July Full Moon could include spells and charms for success, physical work for our bodies (our vessels), and strengthening and expanding our auras.

August: *Sturgeon Moon* (*Fish Moon, Red Moon, Green Corn Moon, Grain Moon, Blueberry Moon*)

The waters are teeming with fish that provide nourishment to many coastal people. Sturgeon, the large fish that fill the Great Lakes, were a bountiful catch at this time of year for the Native American tribes who dwelled on the region's shores. This month is the ideal time to connect with the Water element as fish move deftly through its depths, navigating it with ease. Rituals for the August Full Moon could include ritual swimming or baths, dream work, or psychic ability expansion.

September: *Corn Moon* (*Harvest Moon**, *Fruit Moon, Barley Moon*)

After receiving tireless care since first breaking soil in early Spring, the crops are finally ready to harvest. The corn is sweet, pumpkins round, apples juicy, barley plump, and grapes ready to be pressed. Although the summer moons typically celebrate nature's bounty, this Full Moon honors the direct result of our hard work. We have planted our seeds, nurtured our intentions and watched them grow, risen to challenges, and refined our practice, and now we reap our reward. Summer has come to an end. Rituals for the September Full Moon could include abundance and confidence spells, cooking spells, wine potions, and corn husk doll crafting.

October: *Hunter's Moon* (*Harvest Moon**, *Blood Moon, Falling Leaves Moon, Travel Moon, Dying Moon*)

What once blossomed in the fields has been reaped, and now the deer, fat and sleek, scour the fields for leftovers before the harshness of winter sets in. Hunters lie in wait with their bows and arrows as they, too, prepare themselves for the cold months ahead. There is something here to learn from both sides. Each displays terrific patience, with watchful eyes and sharpened senses. This month is a good time to hunt for what will fill your body and soul during the upcoming winter. Rituals for October's Full Moon could include ancestor work for guidance, meditation, divination work, and animal or spirit guide communication.

November: *Beaver Moon* (*Hunter's Moon, Mourning Moon**, Frost Moon*)

The fallen leaves that were once colorful and vibrant now carpet the late autumn land in a layer of brown. Brisk winds pick up and gray skies hang over barren fields. The beavers busy themselves, building lodges to shelter them from the cold and snow. Trappers hurry to set traps before the swamps freeze in hopes that the fur they harvest will be enough to keep them warm through the winter. It is time to prepare the home for hibernation. Rituals for the November Full Moon could include stocking the home apothecary, cleansing the home and preparing the hearth, letting go of what does not serve you, and protection spells for the home.

December: *Cold Moon* (*Long Nights Moon, Moon Before Yule*)

Winter has finally arrived, and with it come the cold winds and the first snow. All our preparation during the fall will now serve us through this month and those to come. This is the time to slow down—to breathe. To let your body and your mind rest, to rebuild your energy, and to refill your well of magick after all those busy months. Rituals for the December Full Moon could include breath work, candle and fire magick, weaving and knot tying, and crafting elemental snow water.

---

*Harvest Moon: The Harvest Moon is the Full Moon that occurs closest to the fall equinox. In September, two out of three years, this will be in October in the other year. This Full Moon is considered to be the last opportunity to harvest the crops, and it illuminates the fields so that farmers can work long into the night, reaping the last of what they have sown.

**Mourning Moon: The November Moon is sometimes known as the Mourning Moon if it is the last Full Moon before the Winter Solstice.

Solar Magick

As inhabitants of Earth, we live and die by the Sun. But as practitioners of natural witchcraft, we understand that even in death there is rebirth. The power of the Sun lies in the fact that it can bring forth the blossoms that lie dormant under ice and snow and then scorch the soil until it blisters. The very elements themselves are bent to the Sun's will as they change states throughout the seasons: ice melts into water, winds blow warm and wet, wildfires rage across the bush, and the soil bursts forth with bountiful crops.

As the angles of its rays change, the Sun brings hibernation, migration, rainbows, the auroras, shadows, and global warming. It elicits happiness and warmth and can change the color of our skin and ignite cellular mutations. Our circadian rhythm—the internal clock that naturally regulates our sleep cycle—is set to sunrise and sunset. Ruled by the element of Fire, the Sun is the giver of life, bestowing those qualities of strength, fortitude, resilience, productivity, reactivity, joy, and healing on our practice. In traditions in which planets are assigned genders, the Sun corresponds with male qualities, the opposite of the Moon. If the Moon were the Goddess, the Sun would be the God. While Moon magick works with the delicate inner self, Solar magick works with the radiating outer self. But the Sun can be called upon in many of the same ways as the Moon: for instance, charging crystals and tools, making Sun water, ritual Sun bathing, scrying under the sunlight, as well as healing and meditation. Understand, however, that Solar magick will focus your practice on the outer self. Sometimes you must dig deeper to find the true joy that the Sun imparts. Finding a balance between Sun and Moon magick is key to achieving growth of the whole self.

In astrology, the Sun rules the first day of the week (Sunday), is the ruler of the fifth house (the house of love, children, and creativity), is the ruling planet of Leo (the fiery, limelight-loving zodiac sign), and is the basis for our natal signs. In ritual, we use the Sun to guide the direction of our magick around a circle similar to a sundial. A sunwise (deosil or clockwise) direction is used for constructive magick as the Sun brings things into life, whereas widdershins or anti-sunwise (counterclockwise) is used for destructive magick, since with the retreat of the Sun comes death.

Sun Worship

Sun worship was prevalent throughout ancient paganism and was common in ancient Egyptian, Indo-European, and Meso-American cultures. Ancient Egyptians, the first civilization to measure time via solar cycles, worshipped the Sun gods Horus (rising), Ra (noon), and Osiris (setting). Stonehenge, Newgrange, and the Sun Gate at Machu Picchu, too, are thought to have honored our closest star by measuring the solstices.

Solstices: *Winter: December 21*
Summer: June 21

During the course of the year, there are two days that mark the highest and lowest points of the Sun in the sky at noon when the Sun is farthest

from the equator. These are the Summer and Winter Solstices. When the Sun is at its highest in the sky, we celebrate the Summer Solstice and the imminent death of the Sun, also known as the longest day of the year. Upon the completion of the solstice, the days begin to shorten as we angle away from the Sun in our orbit until we reach the Winter Solstice or the longest night of the year. Here, we celebrate the return of the light, since from here in our hemisphere angles back toward the Sun and the days begin to get longer.

In natural witchcraft, we do not only honor each of these solstices with seasonal festivals, but we also use them to distinguish between the two halves of the year for our rituals. The darker half of the year refers to the timespan between the Summer Solstice and the Winter Solstice. While this can certainly be a powerful time for destructive magick, there are many constructive rituals centered around the home and hearth that can be performed, too. Introspection, family bonding, divinatory and psychic ability expansion, kitchen magick, and woven spells are all ideal foci during the darker half of the year. The lighter half of the year refers to the timespan between the Winter Solstice and the Summer Solstice and is a terrific time to focus on all that the Sun brings into our lives. Growth and increasing rituals are particularly powerful here. When planning rituals throughout the year, you can think of the darker half as "nurturing our inner selves" and the lighter half as "nurturing our outer selves."

Equinoxes: *Autumnal: September 21*
Vernal (Spring): March 21

Just as there are two solstices during the course of the year (when the Sun is farthest from the equator), there are two equinoxes that occur when the Sun is closest to the equator. During this time, day and night are of equal length, and we focus on honoring both the light and dark within us. Without each self, we cannot wholly exist. Our shadow self reveals to us the darkest parts of ourselves: We often hide this aspect of ourselves away, but using the equinoxes to embrace it allows us to integrate it into our whole self and to deepen our magickal well. The Autumnal and Vernal Equinoxes are the perfect times to look for the growth available to you and the abundance that lies before you.

As the Sun moves south of the equator into the Southern Hemisphere, the North Pole leans away from the Sun, and we celebrate the Autumnal Equinox. During this time, we acknowledge our inner darkness and let go of the old ways that hamper our growth. As the Sun moves north of the equator into the Northern Hemisphere, the North Pole leans toward the Sun, and we celebrate the Spring or *Vernal* Equinox. During this time, we focus on breathing new life into ourselves and honoring all the growth of which we are capable.

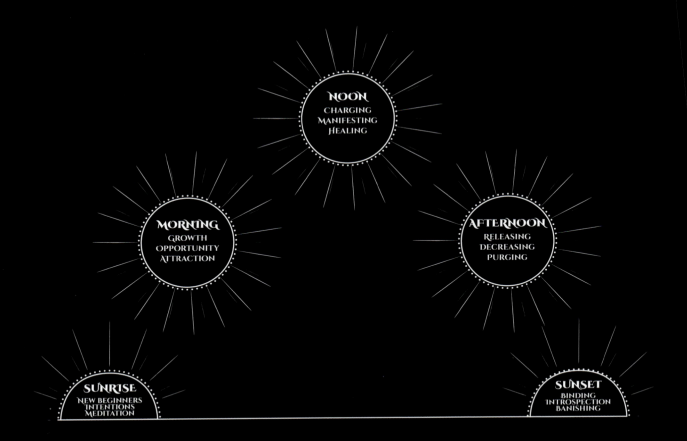

NOON
CHARGING
MANIFESTING
HEALING

MORNING
GROWTH
OPPORTUNITY
ATTRACTION

AFTERNOON
RELEASING
DECREASING
PURGING

SUNRISE
NEW BEGINNERS
INTENTIONS
MEDITATION

SUNSET
BINDING
INTROSPECTION
BANISHING

SPELL TIMING

Timing spells with the Sun not only impart strength and vitality to your rituals, but they also attune your magick with nature's rhythms.

TIME OF DAY
Timing spells and rituals with the phase of the Sun can be compared to moon phase magick.

SUNRISE: *New Moon.* New beginnings, intention-setting, meditation

MORNING: *Waxing Moon.* Growth, prosperity, opportunity, beauty and attraction, relationships

NOON: *Full Moon.* Crystal and magickal tool creating, Sun water, manifesting, healing, divinatory work, spirit communication, abundance, and celebration

AFTERNOON: *Waning Moon.* Releasing old ways, ending toxic relationships, purging

SUNSET: *Dark Moon.* Binding, banishing, meditation, introspection

SOLAR ECLIPSE
A solar eclipse occurs when the Moon passes between the Earth and the Sun and occludes the rays of the Sun. In astrology, this natural phenomenon is treated as an incredibly powerful New Moon, a time for beginnings and endings. Alchemists often view it as an alchemical mar-riage of the Sun and the Moon—a time to call upon the Moon's magick as it mingles with the Sun's. With both luminaries on your side, you can energize transformative rituals that require a level of energy above that of your natural thresh-old, such as quests or spiritual journeys. Then there are those who view a solar eclipse as a timekeeper of sorts, a pause in time during which introspection and time travel to previous or future selves can be accomplished.

Seasonal Festivals

Many neopagan and folk traditions celebrate seasonal festivals according to the annual cycle of the Wheel of the Year. The Wheel is tied to the Sun's cyclical death and rebirth and honors the solstices, equinoxes, and midway points (cross-quarter days) with festivals. Although the festivals are European in origin, the common eightfold Wheel of the Year can be attributed to Gardnerian Wicca (see page 9).

Here, festivals from various cultures (of which none celebrated all eight festivals), some with origins as early as the Stone Age, were arranged into an eight-armed sun cross and given the name *sabbats*. Most modern pagan traditions have adopted this eightfold Wheel, although there are those that only celebrate the quarters (solstices and equinoxes) or festivals from a singular culture. Celtic Reconstructionists, for example, celebrate only the four Gaelic festivals. Similar to the seasonal Full Moons, each seasonal festival has unique magickal correspondences and a set of celebratory rituals. As a natural witch, you should make your own choice as to which seasonal festivals to celebrate. The suggested rituals can be altered to fit your regional observations.

MIDWINTER (YULE)

Ancient Germanic/Christian. December 21 (Winter Solstice)

Although the Winter Solstice is the longest night of the year, it is the celebration of the return of the light and the rebirth of the Sun: Every day from the Winter Solstice until the Summer Solstice will be a little bit longer. This is a festive holiday often marked by grand feasts, tree decorating, gift giving, wassailing (merry making with cider in hand) or caroling, evergreen boughs, mistletoe, mulled wine, spiced cider, bonfires, pomander balls, and a yule log. Traditionally the Yule tree was decorated with fruit and lights to represent all that the ancient pagans hoped would return with the arrival of the solstice.

Yule Log: *A Yule log is a long-held tradition for pagans and Christians alike and symbolizes the re-emergence of light. It brings good tidings, prevents misfortune, and calls festival-goers to circle around it to tell ghost stories and play games.*

1 To begin your own yule log ritual, collect a large piece of wood (traditionally ash) from your land or receive it as a gift from a neighbor or friend. You will want the yule log to burn from evening to morning for at least 12 hours, so choosing the proper log is important: A stump is ideal.

2 Dress the log in evergreens, pinecones, and cranberries, and dust it with yule spices like cloves and nutmeg and a bit of flour. If you have kept a piece of last year's yule log safely under your bed to prevent fire and misfortune from reaching your home, use this to light the new yule log. If not, you can use bayberry matches.

3 If you are able, allow the yule log to smolder for twelve days until after the New Year (otherwise, extinguish the fire in the morning by covering the embers in ash and a layer of baking soda). Once the embers have cooled completely, wrap a piece in a bundle and place it under your bed for next year's lighting.

A modern alternative is to create a yule log with candles. Use a smaller log of ash or white birch and carefully drill three holes into the top of it, large enough to fit twelve-hour taper candles. You can choose the colors of the season red, white, and green—or you may prefer to use all red or all white. Dress the log in the same way as above. If you like, have each person present write their wish on a bay leaf and lay it on top of the log, or burn it in the flames. You can either light this Yule log in the fireplace or in the center of your feasting table.

IMBOLC (IMBOLG, BRIGID'S DAY, CANDLEMAS)
Gaelic. February 1

Originally a pagan festival honoring the Celtic goddess of the hearth, Brigid (the patron of fire, smithcraft, poetry, healing, and childbirth), Imbolc celebrates the quickening of the Earth. It marks the midway point between the Winter Solstice and the Vernal Equinox and brings with it the flowing of milk and preparations for breaking the soil. The Celts welcomed the imminent return of spring with Brigid's crosses made from wheat stalks and straw corn dollies called Brideo'gas, which were given as gifts or exchanged to encourage a prosperous growing season. Homes are cleansed and blessed with a ritual besom, and hearth fires are lit, or candles placed in all of the windows, to welcome the return of the light.

Seed Blessing: *Just before starting your seeds, hold them loosely in a cloth in your hand and chant, "In this soil that we sow, you will take hold and grow."*

VERNAL EQUINOX (OSTARA, ĒOSTRE)
Celtic/Anglo-Saxon/Germanic/Christian. March 21

The spring equinox is a time to celebrate the re-emergence of the fertile land. Day and night are of equal length as the dark and light lie in perfect balance with each other. In some theistic religions, the equinox honors the Anglo-Saxon goddess Ēostre, the goddess of spring. Everything that was planned and blessed during Imbolc is now put to use. Of particular importance to the Vernal Equinox, the nocturnal hare, who is thought to "die" each morning when it retreats to its burrow after a night of activity, represents immortality. Eggs, flowers, and seeds all symbolize the burgeoning of new life across the land. Hot cross buns—spiced

POMANDER BALL

Pomander balls make lovely gifts, decorations, and tree ornaments, and are fun and easy for children to make during the Midwinter festival. Simply take an orange, and route a red ribbon through the center by sticking the point of a wooden skewer into a small fold at the end of the ribbon and pushing it through. Tie a knot on the bottom and a loop on the top, then insert whole cloves into the skin in an array of designs. Dust the orange in a blend of cinnamon, clove, and nutmeg. Now you have a fragrant and natural air freshener that adds to the festivity of the season and repels negative energy (and even moths!) for years to come.

NATURALLY DYED EGGS
❦

1 Gather white or ivory eggs from your backyard, a neighbor, or the local farmer's market and hard-boil them for approximately 11 minutes. Allow them to cool until just warm.

2 Prepare dye baths made from spinach, beets, and purple cabbage by combining 1 quart of water with 2 to 3 tablespoons of white or apple cider vinegar and approximately 4 cups of chopped vegetables. Bring the pots to a boil and let simmer for 30 minutes over low heat.

3 Cool the dyes and strain through a sieve or cheesecloth into bowls. Allow your eggs to sit in each bath for 30 minutes; then remove and dry them on a linen cloth. Bless the eggs with a small intention such as, "May you symbolize the fertility of the land."

buns decorated with crosses for the goddess Ēostre—are a popular recipe during this time.

BELTANE (MAY DAY)
Gaelic. May 1

The ancient Celtic festival of Beltane is celebrated at the midway point between the Vernal Equinox and the Summer Solstice. Beltane is a fire festival that marks the beginning of summer and honors the abundance that fills the Earth. Flowers are bursting, new life is rampant, and growth and renewal abounds. Traditional balefire rites include jumping over the fire for purifying the body and aura and pledging eternal love, as well as dancing, and using the wafting smoke to protect the crops from pests. Red, orange, and yellow flowers, faerie magick, the maypole, and knot or cord magick are common symbols of Beltane. Beltane is one of the two liminal times—the other being Samhain (see page 100)—during which the veil between this world and the next is at its thinnest.

Handfasting: *Used to bind two people together, handfasting is a pagan ceremony with ancient Celtic origins. Traditionally, handfasting was a trial marriage lasting a year and a day that would ultimately determine whether the couple should officially "tie the knot." While there are many variations on the custom, the couple's hands are bound together with a rope made of three cords of different colors: blue for fidelity, red for passion, and white for purity. The rope is wrapped in a way to represent the Celtic knot pattern that symbolizes everlasting unity.*

MIDSUMMER (LITHA)
Anglo-Saxon. June 21 (Summer Solstice)

From here on, the days will grow shorter and shorter until Midwinter arrives with the return of the light. Litha is celebrated in much the same way as Beltane, but during this time we are saying farewell to the Sun and blessing the crops to encourage a bountiful harvest. Celebrations include dancing around a balefire at the top of a hill (symbolizing the Sun at its most powerful) until sunrise on Midsummer's eve, where it is possible to catch a glimpse of the faerie realm. Using the Midsummer ashes as an amulet or sowing them into the fields is thought to offer protection and bounty. An oak tree, the traditional tree of Litha, represents the doorway through which we enter the darker half of the year, and it is decorated with yellow cloth and sunflowers.

Midsummer Fae Garden Party: *Hosting a faerie garden party is a fun Midsummer ritual. Construct a tiny faerie house out of small twigs and bark and adorn it with heather, jasmine, roses, and thyme; play music; make faerie cakes, tea cakes, or other sweets; leave out nectar or juice near the faerie house for them to enjoy; and dance to coax the faeries out from their realm. Be careful to carry the herb rue (see page 129) on you in case the fae become troublesome.*

LUGHNASADH (LAMMAS)
Gaelic/Anglo-Saxon. August 1

Lughnasadh is the first harvest festival of the year and celebrates the heat of Summer, the Celtic Sun-King Lugh, and the reaping of wheat. In Celtic tradition, Lughnasadh was a wake held for the death of Lugh's foster mother, Tailtiu, who cleared the Irish land for farming. In natural witchcraft, we use this festival to hold a wake for the Sun as the Autumnal Equinox looms. During this time, the grain fields are harvested and the first sheaves of wheat are cut and made into loaves of bread, which are eaten later that evening as the hot summer Sun blazes on. In Old English, Lammas translates to "loaf mass."

Lammas Harvest Ritual: *Spend the day outside harvesting the fruits of the gardens, fields, and orchards. As you meander through nature, slowly feasting on your hard-earned bounty, be sure to drop seeds into the earth to see if they sprout the next year, for this festival is all about the cyclical death and rebirth of nature. If you do not have access to your own plot, visit a local farm, fair, or pick-your-own berry farm or orchard. Choose a bare spot in the sun and have a picnic, dispersing the seeds as you feast. Say a little blessing over each seed, such as "Into the earth to be reborn."*

AUTUMNAL EQUINOX (MABON)

Neopagan. September 21

The Autumnal Equinox brings equal length to night and day as we make our slow descent into the darker half of the year. Although this equinox has been celebrated throughout many cultures, Mabon appears to be a construct of neopaganism. It is named after the Welsh God Mabon, who was the son of the Earth mother goddess, Modron. Mabon celebrates the waning of the Sun and the impending completion of nature's cycle. As the second harvest festival of the year, Mabon focuses on the fruit and vegetable harvest as well as a great harvest feast. During this time, we give our thanks for this abundance and focus on preparations for winter. We store food (canning and pickling fresh harvests that will not be consumed at the feast), clear out our pantries and cupboards, and make room for all that that will keep us warm and satiated over the long, cold months ahead. Symbols of Mabon include the cornucopia, apples, pomegranates, wine, nature spirits, and berries. During this time, the veil between this world and the next is starting to thin, so our ancestors are close by.

SAMHAIN (HALLOWEEN, ALL HALLOWS' EVE, HALLOWMAS)

Gaelic. October 31

Samhain celebrates the liminal time between the Autumn Equinox and the Winter Solstice. It is the final harvest festival in the Wheel of the Year, the last of four Gaelic seasonal festivals, and the official end of summer. Like Beltane, it is a fire festival, and large balefires are lit to cleanse and protect the land. During this time, the veil between the physical world and the afterlife is gossamer thin. According to Irish mythology, Samhain is a celebration for the dead, and spirits and fae folk are free to walk around the Earthly realm . . . and, perhaps, to become a little meddlesome in the lives of mortals. Costumes and jack-o-lanterns are thought to be protective measures against such spirits. To honor our ancestors, we create an altar with their photographs and personal effects and attempt to contact them using divination. During the Samhain feast, we leave out a place setting at the table for the dearly departed and offer them their favorite foods. The eve of All Hallows' Eve, also known as Cabbage Night or Mischief Night in the American Northeast and in Northern England, conjures fond memories of my childhood where, for one night of the year, children could act like little "devils" or troublesome spirits, casting mostly harmless pranks about the neighborhood. Traditional symbols of Samhain are pumpkins and gourds, cauldrons, besoms, and apples.

Lighting the Path Ritual: *As the Sun begins to set on Samhain and you are finishing the preparations for your feast, place a single lit candle in every window and a lantern at every entrance to show your ancestors the way home. It is also said that you may leave the back door or a window open so that their spirits may enter.*

MABON APPLE PROTECTION SPELL BAG

1 On the day of the Autumnal Equinox, go apple picking in an orchard or visit a farmer's market. Look for an apple that is large, firm, and of solid red coloring. At your altar or in a space in nature, cleanse and bless the apple and your utility blade (or boline) with apple blossom and cinnamon incense (or sage and bay leaf).

2 Cut the apple in half horizontally across the middle and admire the pentagram of seeds that appears in the middle. Consider its connection with the Spirit element and the universal life force. One by one, dig out the seeds with the tip of your knife and place them in a black silk or linen bag with black tourmaline chips so that the chips themselves resemble the apple seeds and mingle with their protective energy.

3 Bless the bag with a small incantation such as "Protect this home and all that dwell within it," and hang the bag over your hearth or altar. If you like, fashion a small besom from apple tree branches, hang it horizontally above the hearth or entrance to your home, and tie the bag to it.

CHAPTER 7

CRYSTALS & VIBRATIONAL TOOLS

For as long as humankind has walked the Earth, we have treasured the stones forged deep below its surface. In almost supernatural colors and shapes, these crystals come to us through the broken crust of the Earth, feeding our magick with their unique vibrations. Ancient Egyptians used crystals for protection, healing, and safe passage into the afterlife. Greeks and Romans, too, as well as Meso-Americans and many indigenous tribes, understood the immense power these crystals hold.

Although the formation and vibration of crystals can be explained by the laws of physics, their magick lies in our ability to wield them. Using them alone, in grids, or as the centerpiece of a vibrational tool like a wand or talisman can help us to grow and to direct energy to our rituals. Selecting the ideal crystal for the job is something that takes knowledge, familiarity, and intuition.

The best way to attune your magick to the vibrations of crystals is to spend time with them. Cleanse them. Charge them with all the energy the Moon and Sun can muster. Nurture them and they will respond to your every (subatomic) move.

The Science of Crystals

Crystals were born millions of years ago as the Earth's surfaces shifted, pushing them to the surface through cracks in its crust. Once discovered, they were revered for the immense power they imparted to the bearer. Over 4,000 minerals have been discovered here on Earth and they comprise the many variations of crystals we use in our practice.

Interestingly enough, though, it is the structure of a crystal that defines it and gives it shape: Diamonds and graphite have the same chemical composition and differ only in their structure. It is here, in their internal geometry, in combination with their chemical composition and color influence, that each crystal's unique vibratory influence is determined. Although science considers only those formations with crystalline structures to be crystals, in witchcraft we use the term to encompass any naturally formed object capable of storing and transmitting vibrational energy. These can include those natural objects that were used in ancient times, such as bones, shells, fossils, pearl, jet; and resins, such as amber.

Vibrations

The use of crystals in witchcraft is based on the universal law that every object here on Earth has a unique vibration. Not only do these crystalline structures emit their own vibration, but they also store, transmit, and resonate energy. Because crystals act as mediums through which energy travels, they are used in everything from computer processors to quartz watches. Quartz and other piezoelectric crystals contain an electric charge that is stored as potential energy inside their lattice structures. Even in nonpiezoelectric crystals, atoms are creating wavelike propagations of vibrations that carry heat, scatter electrons, and interact with light.

STANDING POINT

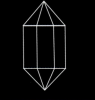

DOUBLE TERMINATED

GENERATOR

RECORDKEEPER

CLUSTER

PHANTOM

TWIN

INCLUSION

RUTILATED

Formations

Crystals are typically formed under extreme pressure and temperature as atoms rearrange to compose their highly stable structures. Here is the process that creates crystals: Under high temperature, a combination of minerals is suspended in water or molten rock. When that fluid is pushed through the cavities between the Earth's mantle and crust, it becomes cool enough for the minerals to form crystals, which are then either pushed to the Earth's surface by volcanic activity or mined. New layers may be added to the crystals along their way to the surface, or they may be subject to changing conditions or growth interruptions, or they may be formed inside gas bubbles: Factors like these may result in several of the formations below.

INCLUSION: A different, smaller crystal or mineral that is encapsulated inside a larger one. Contains the qualities of the original stone (often quartz) as well as its own vibrations.

ELESTIAL CRYSTAL: Has multiple points coming off the crystal body. Provides a direct link to the spiritual realm and can transmit spiritual vibrations to the receiver.

PHANTOM: A transparent crystal that appears as a ghost encapsulated inside a larger transparent crystal. Emits powerful cleansing and healing energies.

RECORDKEEPER CRYSTALS: Triangles etched on one or more faces. Contains a direct link to the etheric realm and the Akashic Hall of Records.

RUTILATED CRYSTAL: Formed when impurities crystallize inside a host crystal. Illuminates the areas to focus on for spiritual growth.

TWIN CRYSTAL: Two crystal points that are joined together side by side. Assists in building and attracting relationships.

Shapes

Both natural and carved shapes can be used to enhance the properties of a crystal or facilitate to the way in which you will use it.

CLUSTER: Natural formation of many points originating from a base. Radiates a high level of energy that is excellent for cleansing negative energy. Acts as a charging bed for other crystals.

DOUBLE TERMINATED: Contains two faceted ends or *terminations* that can release and transmit energy at the same time. Used for divinatory work (to send and receive messages) as well as dream recall and healing.

PYRAMID: Anchors energy at the base and transmits it from the apex. Along with standing points, pyramid crystals are excellent for energy amplification and are often used as center stones on grids.

SPHERE: Emits energy in all directions. Used for scrying and healing.

STANDING POINT (TOWER): A carved or naturally formed point that has been leveled on the bottom. A very powerful energizer that can amplify and direct energy, particularly if in a *generator* shape (in which six equal faces meet at a central point at the apex).

TUMBLED STONE: Makes for an easy traveler, as it is small and convenient enough to carry in your pocket. Radiates gentle energy in all directions.

WAND: Sharpened or rounded at one or both ends. Used to direct or channel energy to an intention.

Common Crystals Used in Natural Witchcraft

In our practice, we use crystals to cleanse our sacred space, charge our magickal tools, direct energy to our rituals, and protect our vessel and magick from malefic forces. Although a boundless world of crystals is available to us, a relatively small number of them will see us through most spell types. Each of the following crystals was chosen for its unique properties, all of which can assist you in honing your craft. However, you are free to seek stones beyond this list to find those that resonate with your chosen path.

Amethyst: *Purple/Violet Quartz. Aquarius and Pisces.* ♃ ♆ △ ▽

Once used by the Greeks as protection against drunkenness, amethyst is a stone that brings serenity and gentle healing to the bearer. Its soothing energy relieves stress, promotes peaceful sleep, and provides psychic protection while opening your mind's eye and enhancing spiritual awareness in lucid dreaming, astral travel, and spirit communication. Amethyst connects the physical plane with higher realms, raising energy into the crown and third eye chakras.

SUGGESTED SUBSTITUTIONS: *Fluorite, howlite, lapis lazuli, moonstone, labradorite*

Black Tourmaline (Schorl): *Black Borosilicate. Capricorn.* ♄ ▽

Used in ancient times as a protection talisman, schorl acts as a psychic shield with the ability to transmute negative energy into positive energy. This piezoelectric crystal has two polar ends and

is considered to be the most powerful stone for protection in rituals as well as against psychic attack and negative environmental energy. Grid around your sacred space or home or carry on your body away from the skin for protection and grounding.

SUGGESTED SUBSTITUTIONS: *Onyx, hematite, obsidian, smoky quartz*

Blue Kyanite: *Blue Aluminosilicate. Aries, Taurus, Libra, Capricorn.* ☿ △ ▽

Blue Kyanite is known as the Stone of Alignment and is one of the few crystals that does not need to be cleansed due to its high vibration and inability to absorb negative energy. It promotes inner balance, gentle healing, clarity of thought, and honest communication. Kyanite is best used in learning your truth through the gentle exploration of your psyche and raising your energy to higher planes through meditation.

SUGGESTED SUBSTITUTION: *Jade*

Carnelian: *Orange/Orange-Red Chalcedony. Leo, Virgo, Aries.* ☉ ♂ △

Used by ancient Egyptians and alchemists in the Middle Ages, Carnelian has been dubbed the Stone of Action. It has a bold energy and encourages confidence, courage, motivation, and physical power. Carnelian's association with blood and the Fire element enhances vigor, virility, and passion. It can be used to cleanse other crystals.

SUGGESTED SUBSTITUTIONS: *Red garnet, ruby*

Citrine: *Yellow Quartz. Leo and Aries.* ☉ △

Sunny citrine brings joy, happiness, opportunity, prosperity, abundance, healing, and the power of manifestation. Its warmth and light creates fertile fields for growth in business or financial ventures and spreads positive energy. Citrine is selfcleansing.

SUGGESTED SUBSTITUTIONS: *Yellow sapphire, yellow topaz, sunstone, amber*

Clear Quartz: *Silicon Dioxide. All.* ☉ ☽ △ ▽

Originally thought to be ice by the Greeks, quartz is one of the most abundant minerals in the world. Its piezoelectric vibrations can be used for clarity, manifestation, and imprinting of intention. As a generator, quartz amplifies the energy of other crystals and broadcasts it throughout the physical and metaphysical realms. Clear quartz is a Master Healer and works to clear and purify the energy around it. Because of this, clusters are often used as beds for cleansing tools and other crystals. Quartz points excel at opening channels for energy flow and transmuting light into energy.

SUGGESTED SUBSTITUTION: *Selenite*

Copper: *Metal. Taurus and Libra.* ♀ ▽

While it is not considered to be a crystal by scientific definition, copper is quite useful in magickal workings as a conductor of energy. Copper dowsing rods are often used to locate water.

Fluorite: *Calcium Fluoride. Capricorn and Pisces.* ☿ △ ▽

Fluorite is a balancing stone known for harmonizing spiritual energy, cleansing and nurturing the aura, and neutralizing stress.

SUGGESTED SUBSTITUTIONS: Amethyst, lapis lazuli, howlite, rose quartz

Green Aventurine: *Green Quartz. Libra, Virgo, Aries.* ☿ ▽

Known as the Good Luck Stone, green aventurine brings luck, prosperity, abundance, and success to the bearer. It calms and opens the mind and encourages focus on gratitude and attracting opportunity. It is best used in spells to attract money as amulets in honey jars, cash boxes and registers, or in the pockets of those seeking success in gambling.

SUGGESTED SUBSTITUTIONS: *Jade, malachite, pyrite, citrine*

Labradorite: *Plagioclase Feldspar. Scorpio, Sagittarius, Leo.* ♃ ♆ ▽

The native people of Canada believed labradorite, often called the Stone of Destiny, to be frozen fire that fell from the Northern Lights. Its vibrations can awaken magick, boost psychic abilities, ease existential crises, and connect you with your true purpose on a spiritual journey to higher realms.

SUGGESTED SUBSTITUTIONS: *Amethyst, lapis lazuli*

Lapis Lazuli: *Metamorphic Rock. Sagittarius and Capricorn.* ♀ △ ▽

Lapis lazuli has a mystical past as the stone used in the protective Eye of Horus of the ancient Egyptians. It promotes wisdom, good judgment, truth, memory retention, and open communication. Because it activates the third eye and balances the throat chakra, it allows us to see and speak clearly, and it also aids in divination.

SUGGESTED SUBSTITUTIONS: *Amethyst, azurite, turquoise*

Moonstone: *Feldspar. Cancer.* ☽ ▽

The ancient Romans believed that Moonstone was formed by solidified moonrays. Indeed, it brings the powers of the Moon to the bearer: intuition, psychic expansion, emotional balancing, and illumination of danger ahead.

SUGGESTED SUBSTITUTIONS: Amethyst, labradorite, lapis lazuli

Rose Quartz: *Pink Quartz. Libra and Taurus.* ♀ ▽

Rose Quartz is the Stone of Beauty and Love. It bestows comfort, love, healing, romance, empathy, and forgiveness upon the bearer. It is best used in rituals for selflove, hearthealing, clearing blockages in the heart, nourishing the spirit, soothing anxiety or depression, and healing from trauma, loss, grief, or crises. Rose quartz should be worn against the skin.

SUGGESTED SUBSTITUTION: *Fluorite*

Selenite: *Gypsum. Cancer.* ☽ ▽

As the Stone of Clarity and Insight, Selenite radiates light and connects you to spirits in the etheric realm. It emits purity, honesty, and positivity, and it allows energy to flow like liquid. Selenite is best used in divination and spirit communication, meditation, lucid dreaming, and astral travel, and it can be used to clear and charge other crystals and magickal tools. Note that it is not a mineral and will dissolve in water.

SUGGESTED SUBSTITUTIONS: *Desert rose, clear quartz*

Cleansing and Charging Crystals

Every relationship between individuals begins with a spark. A meeting of two energetic beings who share similar intentions. But if this relationship is to be successful, it must be nurtured. Negativity must be purged, communication must flow freely, and work must be put in. Similarly, when you first hold a crystal, a relationship begins. You activate the crystal, tuning into it with your magick and leaning on it for the unique energy it imparts to your craft. But, like any relationship, crystal magick relies upon give and take. If we ask a crystal to absorb negative energy, we must then cleanse it.

If we channel energy through a crystal for our own purposes, we must allow it time to return to its natural frequency. If we want a crystal to understand us, we must tell it what we want. This is the key to casting a lifetime of spells with crystals by our sides.

Each crystal has a unique vibrational frequency that can be affected by negative energy or high-energy events. When you choose a crystal to add to your practice, you will want to cleanse it of any accumulated energy and charge it to restore it to its natural frequency state. Crystal cleansing and charging should also be done after most rituals—unless you are creating amulets or talismans, in which case you can develop a crystal care routine that aligns with your practice. You will be able to observe if a crystal needs care because it will have a dull, lifeless appearance or a feeling of low energy when you hold it. Charging a crystal restores it to its natural frequency state and gives you the opportunity to program it with your intention if you so choose. There are a few methods for cleansing and charging crystals, most of which can be dual-purpose.

Crystals

There are several crystals that are thought to be capable of both selfcleansing and cleansing other crystals. These are citrine, kyanite, and selenite.

Earth

Bury your crystals in the soil for twenty-four hours to retune the crystal with the pulse of nature.

Full Moonlight

Place the crystal under the light of the Full Moon and allow it to cleanse and charge for at least two to three hours. If you are able, leave it out for the evening, but be sure to retrieve it before Sunrise.

Noon Sunlight

Place the crystal in full view of the Noon Sun for one to two hours. Be sure to choose another method for those crystals whose colors fade in sunlight: amethyst, citrine, fluorite, green aventurine, rose quartz, smokey quartz, and more.

Light

After cleansing, hold the crystal in your hands and visualize a bright light traveling from your fingertips into the crystal. As it enters the crystal, the crystal emanates a glow from the inside out until it is activated and awakened. Program your intention with an incantation, such as "I honor your power to heal the heart," in the example of rose quartz.

Salt

Place the crystal on a bed of sea salt and leave it there for twenty-four hours. Be sure to discard the salt afterward, as it has now absorbed negative energy from the crystal.

Smoke

Pass burning sage, sweet grass, palo santo, copal, myrrh, frankincense, or any of the ancient resins over your crystals to cleanse them.

Spring Water

In the Noon Sun or under the Full Moon, allow water from a spring, brook, river, or other natural, flowing water source to run over and cleanse the crystal. You can also do this in a bowl of spring water in your backyard or lit window. Be wary of crystals that degrade in water or that should not be placed in water for other reasons: amber, kyanite, moonstone, selenite, and more.

Time

Given enough time, crystals will return to their natural and stable frequency states. Place the crystal in a safe spot and check on it from time to time: Once it has reclaimed its luster, it is ready to complement your magick once again.

Tuning Fork or Singing Bowl

Allow the vibrations from the tuning fork or singing bowl to penetrate the crystal and retune it to its natural state.

How Crystals Shape Our Magick

There are many ways to invite crystals into our practice. In addition to shaping them into vibrational tools, we can carry them in our pockets as amulets; we can align them with chakras and make grids on our altars; or we can simply include them in our rituals as focal points and energy centers.

Carrying Crystals with Us

Carrying a crystal in your pocket or a charm bag is one of the easiest ways to incorporate crystal magick into your practice. An easy-to-carry raw or tumbled stone can make the ideal amulet both for short-term purposes, like luck in an interview, or for long-term purposes, like protection against psychic attack. Because we receive energy on the left side of the body, *the receiving side*, you will want to carry stones for attraction of forces and protection from incoming energies in your left pocket. The right side of the body is the *acting side*, from which you emit energy, so you will want to carry stones for confidence, outer strength, or any other external qualities you seek to embody in your right pocket. Healing crystals, however, like rose quartz and citrine, should be worn against the skin to direct the healing vibrations inward. Keep in mind that you will need to develop a crystal care schedule for the stones that take up daily residence in your pocket or on your skin. A simple routine such as placing your crystals on a bedside selenite charging plate every evening to cleanse and charge while you sleep can accompany the monthly Full Moon crystal care routine (see page 113).

Chakra Healing

Although we have not focused on chakras individually in this book, there are many witches who honor them as energy centers in the body. When activated and aligned, they can assist you in energizing and balancing each of these energy

GRID INTENTIONS

❧

To be used in intuitive patterns on your altar or in your home.

HEALING: Rose quartz, clear quartz, jasper, and calendula

JOY: Citrine, amber, sunstone, and daisies or sunflower petals

LOVE: Rose quartz, moonstone, amethyst, and rose petals

PROSPERITY: Green aventurine, pyrite, citrine, and lucky coins

PROTECTION: Black tourmaline, obsidian, selenite, and black salt

centers as well as reaching the higher planes of consciousness. Each crystal has a chakra or set of chakras with which it resonates, and can be placed on the body as singular crystals or in grids.

Crystal Grids

Often used for manifesting specific desires or goals, crystal grids harness the energy of different crystals in unison. Gridded crystals are chosen for their ability to work together toward a common intention and are often placed in *sacred geometry*. Together they create a shift in energy that helps to manifest your goal or protect a space. Grids can be large enough to surround your home or small enough to fit on the palm of your hand.

Designing a grid can seem overwhelming, but you need not follow sacred geometry or any of the complexities that are popular in modern grid work. Crystal gridding can be an entirely intuitive process. You may choose to use a crystal grid template on a cloth, copper plate, or wooden board, or you can design your own shapes based on your intention. However, there are a few things that should be taken into account when designing your grid. Before placing your crystals on the grid, it is good to cleanse and charge them with your intention, paying special attention to the master crystal in the center. The master crystal is usually a standing crystal point meant to direct energy upward to the Spirit element. After gridding your crystals, you can then activate the grid with a clear quartz generator or point by charging each one in a clockwise direction from the outermost crystals to the master crystal while chanting your intention.

Sacred Geometry works with the belief that the existence of repeating geometrical patterns in nature implies that the world is a product of design. In natural witchcraft, we operate under the assumption that sacred geometry is a law of the natural universe based on the intertwining relationship between the elements. Observed in natural occurrences, such as crystals themselves, honeycombs, and chambered nautilus shells, sacred geometry has been symbolized in ancient geometric designs like the Seed of Life, the Flower of Life, the Tree of Life, the Lotus, and the ouroboros. Each shape in sacred geometry has a symbolic meaning and can be used as a building block for manifesting energy through a grid. While your intuition should guide you to create the grid that is right for your particular intention, you can create a grid in the pattern of one of these geometric designs to aid your intention, if you like.

Creating Vibrational Tools with Crystals: Talismans, Amulets, and Wands

Throughout every culture, ancient alchemists have transformed simple earthly matter into powerful vibrational tools for healing and protection. Not only do these tools impart their power to the bearer, but they are also a convenient way to carry spells and direct energy. In our practice, crystals can be enchanted and worn as charms, talismans, or amulets, or fashioned into wands and scepters for ritual use.

TALISMANS

The earliest known crystal talisman appeared during the Upper Paleolithic period, around the same time as the origins of witchcraft, and was made of Baltic amber. Talismans are created in ritual with crystals or other objects to bestow the wearer with some magickal power. Their creation generally draws power from sources such as the planets, elements, sigils, or sacred geometry to attract or generate specific aspects, like love, luck, beauty, and protection. Sometimes a talisman can be a sigil itself, or a seal stamped or carved into copper or another metal, and can be hung or hidden in the home. The important distinction between a talisman and an amulet is that a talisman is charged with the magick of the creator while an amulet is naturally enchanted.

Charisma Talisman: *To be used to bestow confidence and charm upon the wearer. Best performed under the Morning Sun under the influence of the Sun.*

1 Paint or etch the symbol for the Sun on a gold backing on a gold setting tray for a pendant or cabochon while repeating the following incantation: "Activate charisma and confidence."

2 Place the talisman in a cotton bag of lemon balm, cloves, and St. John's wort and allow it to charge until the Noon Sun.

3 Remove the talisman from the bag and hang it from a carnelian-beaded cord so that you can wear it at the level of your solar plexus (just above your belly button), the chakra for confidence. Cleanse and recharge under the Noon Sun.

HAGSTONE

Also called an adder stone or hex stone, a hagstone has a naturally formed hole through its center. Hagstones are thought to ward off malefic forces, protect the home and land, peer into the faerie realm, increase fertility, and heal all manner of afflictions, including snake bites.

In northern Germany, hagstones were thought to be formed of a mass of twisting serpents whose venom had eaten away a hole in the center. Other parts of old Europe considered it to be protection against the "evil hag" spirit that afflicted many a home, and it would often be worn by cun-ning folk to ward against the evil eye. To use it as a protection amulet, you can tie a cord through the hole and wear it around your neck. It can also be hung in your home, on bedposts to ward off nightmares, or on an object you would like to protect.

AMULETS

Amulets are naturally enchanted objects that often ward off baneful energy. They can consist of a simple stone such as a crystal or a hagstone carried or worn on the body, or a symbolic object such as a rabbit's foot, a horseshoe, or a lucky coin.

WANDS

A wand is a vibrational tool that helps to direct energy during a ritual. It can be as simple as a piece of wood or selenite, or it can be an ornately carved object with powerful symbols and herbal or crystal inclusions. Selenite and clear quartz wands are particularly useful in casting circles of protection or clearing energy from your sacred space.

Magick Wand: *To be used in rituals for directing energy.*

1 Collect a free fallen branch from a tree such as oak, ash, cherry, birch, or any hard wood that speaks to you. Ensure that it is not rotting or home to insects. Select a branch that is approximately the same shape and size of the wand you envision.

Leave an offering of gratitude at the base of the tree such as water, soil, or compost or natural fertilizer like wood ash.

2 Cleanse the branch of negative energy using your preferred method. Focus on the intention you would like the wand to assist you with and carry it with you throughout the wand-making process.

3 Using your utility blade, scrape the bark off of the branch and begin to carve it into a wand. Once it is the shape and size you desire, sand the wand until smooth.

4 Carve an indentation into the top of the wand. Choose a crystal based on the properties that match your intention and place it in the indentation, affixing it with copper wire or leather cord that you wrap around the base until it is stable at the top of the wand.

5 Charge the wand with your preferred method. It is now ready to use in ritual.

CHAPTER 8

HERBALISM FOR MAGICK

In today's society, we tend to think of plants as the pretty things that adorn our windows, the greenery that dots our footpaths, and the blooms that beckon us with their colorful petals. We forget that, before modern medicine came along with its plastic bottles and childproof caps, nature itself was medicine. The mortar and pestle was a laboratory; the cauldron, a beaker on a hot plate; and the forest, a pharmaceutical factory.

We forget that plants, too, carry vibrational medicine that heals our psyche and feeds our magick. That each plant is alive, growing, and transforming and creating life.

As witches and sorcerers, we use ritual to coax out medicine and energy from plants. With every plant we come to know, we build our own herbal repertoire. Our *materia medica* become filled with sketches and notes. Bottle by bottle, salve by salve, our apothecary shelves begin to overflow with magickal remedies—testaments to all the energy we have poured into our craft. Herbalism is the study of botany for medicinal and magickal purposes, but, more than that, it is the understanding that every plant contains the power of life itself.

The Magick of Plants

Each plant is part of the life force that abounds—from the birds that pluck the berries from the bushes, to the wind that carries the seed, to the soil through which roots spread and absorb water and nutrients, and to the Sun that radiates energy to feed the plant. Although we may not think of plants as sentient beings, perhaps we need only to learn their language. *Phototropism*, the term describing the movement of plants toward the sunlight, is just one example of how plants respond to their environment.

Some reactions occur instantly, like the Venus flytrap closing its outer leaves around an insect, or the mimosa plant furling up its leaves in response to touch. Other movements happen so slowly that they are imperceptible to the naked eye. If you play music to a telegraph plant and record its movement over time, you will see it "dancing" as you speed through the video. Even touching or caressing a plant can launch a series of physiological reactions that affect its growth.

Because plants do not have eyes, they rely on vibrations to sense and respond to the world around them. These vibrations are what we tune into when we practice herbal magick. Just as with crystals, each plant has a unique "face" or vibratory makeup that is associated with a magickal purpose.

Common Herbal Allies

In the mid-1600s, botanist and physician Nicholas Culpeper combined his knowledge of herbal medicine and astrology and published his findings in the *Complete Herbal* (1653). Although his work remains a vital part of the herbalist's library, we can also intuitively assign astrological properties to herbs, based on their individual natures. The following is a list of common herbal allies in witchcraft along with their Western elemental correspondences, planetary rulers, and suggested magickal uses. These attributes, as well as habitat, appearance, and healing abilities, are used to assign an herb its correspondences. For example, because calendula has bright yellow and orange flowers that have a strong scent, grows strong and quick through the height of the Summer in full Sun, and is used in healing, happiness, and manifestation rituals, it corresponds to the element of Fire and calls the Sun its planetary ruler.

AGRIMONY: ♃ △ Distance healing, reversing psychic attacks or hexes, banishing

ANGELICA: ☉ △ Angel communication, blessing, dispelling negative energy, reversing hexes

APPLE: ♀ ♃ ▽ ▽ Fertility, love, healing, immortality

ASH: ☉ ♃ △ Wand making, besom handles

BASIL: ♂ △ Luck, prosperity, peace

BAY: ☉ △ Intention setting, cleansing stagnant or unwanted energy

BIRCH: ☉ △ Protection, rebirth, renewal

BERGAMOT: ☉ △ Attracting money and success, balance, joy

BORAGE: ♃ △ Quelling melancholy, bringing comfort and cheer

BLUE LOTUS: ☽ ▽ Mild sedative for lucid dreaming, astral travel, spirit communication, divination

BURDOCK: ♀ ▽ Protection, warding

CALENDULA: ☉ △ Happiness, love, healing

CARDAMOM: ♀ ▽ Love, warmth, stimulating, clarifying, calming

CEDAR: ☉ △ ▽ Cleansing, protection, preservation, longevity, ancestral work, wood for wands

CHAMOMILE: ☉ ▽ Luck, prosperity, tranquility

CINNAMON: ☉ △ Passion, desire, spirit communication, divination, protection, clairvoyance

CINQUEFOIL: ☿ △ Divination, dreamwork, astral travel

CLARY SAGE: ☽ ▽ Divination, clairvoyance, meditation, opening third eye

CLOVE: ♃ △ Luck, prosperity, desire, protection from negative energies

COMFREY: ♄ ▽ ▽ Money drawing, protection of self and money while traveling

CYPRESS: ♄ ▽ △ Protection, rebirth

DAMIANA: ♀ ♃ △ Divination, meditation, sleep, lucid dreaming, sex magick

ELDER: ♀ ▽ Blessing, healing, protection, banishing, faerie magick

EYEBRIGHT: ☉ △ Third-eye opening, prophetic dreams, clarity, seeing truth

FENNEL: ☿ △ Memory aid, awakening magick, fertility, protection

FEVERFEW: ♀ ▽ Protection from psychic attack or hexes/curses, healing broken hearts, breaking binding love spells

HAWTHORN: ♂ △ Protection from spirits, negative energy, and black magick spells

HEATHER: ♀ ▽ Luck, faerie magick, love, friendship, opening portals

JASMINE: ☽ ▽ Prophecy, lucid dreaming, divination, pure and true love

JUNIPER: ☉ ☿ ♃ △ Purification, protection against negative energy, hexes, and theft

LAVENDER: ☿ △ Sleep, dreams, serenity, love, purification, clarity

LEMON BALM: ☉ ▽ Antianxiety, success, healing

LEMONGRASS: ☿ △ Cleansing, healing, fidelity

LILAC: ♀ △ Love, meditation, faerie magick

MARSH MALLOW: ♀ ▽ Spirit communication, protection

MEADOWSWEET: ♃ △ Balance, harmony, love, beauty

MUGWORT: ☽ ♀ ▽ Lucid dreaming, astral travel, divination, protection against psychic attacks, past life regression

NETTLE: ♂ △ Protection, hex breaking

OAK: ♃ ▽ Fertility, immortality, protection

ORANGE: ☉ △ Happiness, joy, energizing, uplifting (useful in astral projection)

PATCHOULI: ♄ ▽ Grounding, fertility

PINE: ♂ △ Cleansing, protection

ROSE: ♀ ♃ ▽ Love, beauty, healing, nurturing

ROSEMARY: ☉ △ Memory aid, attraction, remembrance, cleansing, blessing

ROWAN (MOUNTAIN ASH): ☉ △ Protection, success, wand making

SAGE: ♃ ♀ ▽ △ Cleansing, purifying

SANDALWOOD: ☽ ♀ ▽ ♃ Protection, meditation, spirit communication (high vibration)

STAR ANISE: ♃ △ Psychic ability, lucid dreaming

ST. JOHN'S WORT: ☉ △ Rebirth, renewal, repelling negative energy

THYME: ♀ ▽ Faerie magick, joy, positivity

VERVAIN: ♀ ▽ Protection from negative energy, divination, spirit communication, purification

VETIVER: ♄ ▽ Tranquility, grounding

WILLOW: ☽ ▽ Wand making, balance, resonance, harmony

WITCH HAZEL: ☉ △ Divining rods (dowsing), protection

YARROW: ♀ △ Protection (tethers life force to physical world during astral travel)

Poisonous Plants

There are several baneful herbs in the witches' apothecary that are considered toxic and should be handled with care. These are deadly nightshade (*atropa belladonna*), datura, foxglove, hemlock, henbane, mandrake, rue, wolfsbane, and wormwood. Most make for excellent protection allies (particularly rue and mandrake) or are sedative and hallucinogenic as traditional ingredients in Flying Ointment (see below), an ointment used by ancient witches for hedge riding. You may use flower essences to include their energies in your rituals, if you choose; however, it is best to use them in symbolic ways or as physical barriers of protection outside the home until you become intimately acquainted with their unique requirements.

Resins

Resins are sticky, gummy substances exuded from trees and some woody plants in response to injury. They contain powerful medicinal and energetic benefits. Because their purpose is to protect the tree at the site of a wound, most resins can be used in cleansing and protection rituals and are often burned as loose incense. Resin oils can also be made by grinding the resin and infusing it into oil with heat.

AMBER: ☉ △ Protection, ancestral work, Akashic recordkeeper

BENZOIN: ☉ △ Purification, harmony, luck

COPAL: ☉ △ Cleansing, simulating

DRAGON'S BLOOD: ♂△ Passion, action, desire

FRANKINCENSE: ☉ △ △ Cleansing, purification, third-eye opening

MYRRH: ☽ ♃ ▽ Meditation, spirit communication

PALO SANTO: ♀☿ △▽ Meditation, purification, connection to the Spirit element

Salts

Most salts are used in rituals for protection, purification, and blessing due to their association with the Earth element. They can be formed into a physical barrier around your sacred space, sprinkled along thresholds, or placed in bowls on your altar. A few of the commonly used salts in witchcraft are black salt, Dead Sea salt, and pink Himalayan salt.

WITCHES' FLYING OINTMENT

It has been said that, to fly, ancient witches concocted an ointment from poisonous plants such as deadly nightshade, hemlock, and wolfsbane along with the fat of a newborn baby. They then smeared it on the handles of their broomsticks and flew away naked into the night. Today Flying Ointment is used for hedge riding or astral travel and is often made from milder psychoactive thujone-containing herbs such as wormwood and mugwort. (Human sacrifices need not be made for the ointment to be effective!)

From Harvest to Potion: Extracting Magick

To soak in the power of plants, you need only spend time in their presence. Walk within a field of wildflowers and feel the freedom and tenacity of their existence lift your toes. Or seek shade under the canopy of a great oak and abide in the ancient wisdom it shares through the groaning of its gnarled limbs. Bringing this magick into your home apothecary can enhance your craft and empower even the simplest rituals.

Harvesting Tools

Along with a love of wildcrafting, extracting magick from the fields and forest requires just a few tools. If you do not have access to the outdoors, growing herbs in pots, purchasing them at the farmer's market, or ordering dried herbs from reputable online sources are all wonderful alternatives (and no less magickal).

WORK TABLE OR ALTAR: This could be as simple as a cutting board that you place on the kitchen counter or as elaborate as a large stone table in a sacred space. If you prefer to work your herbal magick outdoors, you may choose a hidden spot among the trees where a large stump acts as an enchanted workspace. Or your outdoor space could be an old shed, a picnic blanket, or even your cutting board placed on a balcony surrounded by potted herbs. All that is necessary is that you ensure the surface on which you work herbal magick is used only for that purpose and that it is both physically and spiritually cleansed before each session.

HARVESTING BLADE: For harvesting herbs, I prefer to use a sickle or a harvesting knife, both of which have similarly curved shapes to the Wiccan boline. I also bring a pocket knife that I keep only for lifting resins off bark. As you harvest each plant, take a moment to express your gratitude and intention for the offering. Something simple like "Thank you, soothing lavender, for this gift of serenity" will work just fine.

HARVESTING BASKET: Pack baskets are one of the most helpful items to have on hand when harvesting, especially if you find yourself on a long and winding path. They fit easily on your back and are made of sturdy, woven wood (usually ash). I also like to bring along several cotton cloths to wrap herbs in, as well as a few small glass jars for resins. If you cannot get your hands on a pack basket, any basket with handles or even an old backpack will do.

Harvesting with the Moon

Harvesting herbs from their natural habitats, or *wild harvesting*, is often done in ritual to increase the energetic strength of the plant. Farmers and herbalists alike understand that the Moon's pull on the Earth affects not just the water content of the plant but also the energetic properties of different plant parts. Under a Waxing Moon, magick-minded herbalists harvest those plant parts that are above ground. Here the Moon expands, and its gravitational force pulls away from the Earth,

drawing energies to the top of the plant. During the Waning Moon, we harvest those plant parts that are buried deep within the soil. Here the Moon decreases, and its gravitational force pushes down on the Earth, driving energies to the root of the plant. The sign of the Moon may be used in conjunction with the phase: Air and Fire signs are the best times to harvest, as they are considered barren or infertile signs and growth will have ceased. *The Old Farmer's Almanac* is an excellent resource to have for quick access to the year's moon signs and phases.

Wild Harvesting

When wild harvesting, it is important to be conscientious of the plants you are harvesting. Be sure that they are not endangered or illegal to harvest (black cohosh and sandalwood, for instance, are on the endangered list in many regions), or that you do not remove so much that you kill the plant or destroy the habitat or food source of native wildlife. On your journey, be sure to bring along a local field guide so that you may properly identify each plant. If you are unsure about the accuracy of any of your identifications, it is better to err on the side of caution and leave the plant be. This is particularly true for berries and mushrooms. I often take my young son with me on wild-harvesting trips, and, as we walk, we repeat a couple sayings to keep us safe. "Gills kill" is the phrase most often shouted along our wooded path, because although not all mushrooms with gills are deadly, most of the deadly species do have gills. Another is "Aggregate fruit, down the chute!" Aggregate berries are clusters of tightly packed fruits like raspberries, blackberries, and salmonberries and are almost always safe to eat. White and yellow berries, however, are almost always poisonous; half of all red berries are poisonous; and while only 10 percent of blue,

black, or purple berries are poisonous, those that are (like deadly nightshade berries) can prove fatal. A helpful mnemonic for remembering the "berry rule" comes to us from survival expert Mykel Hawke: "White and yellow, kill a fellow. Purple and blue, good for you. Red: could be good, could be dead." Shiny leaves and milky sap are also often a telltale sign that a plant is poisonous. If you find that a poisonous plant calls to you, or, perhaps, that you have great use for it (rue is a favorite of mine for protection), then be sure to use gloves when harvesting and use it only for symbolic purposes. Take care not to burn it or make any topical or ingestible preparations from it.

Drying Herbs

Once you have harvested your herbs from either the great outdoors or your garden, you will want to dry them to increase their shelf life. You can do this by grouping them into small bunches and hanging them from the beams of a barn or spreading them out on drying racks or old window screens in a dark, warm space. Once they are sufficiently dry, you can bring down the bundles during the Waning Moon (as this is when energies are pushed inward) and store them in glass jars with airtight lids. Be sure to label the containers with the name of the herb and the harvest date and place.

Crafting Herbal Magick

Now lining the shelves of your apothecary are glass jars of beautifully dried herbs just waiting to release their potential energy to your magick. Processing the herbs for magickal preparations should be done in ritual under the influence of the cosmos. You may work with the moon phases as well as the astrological planetary hours that we learned about in Chapter 5 (see page 71). If you choose to work with the Moon, a Full or Waxing Moon is the ideal time to prepare and decant your preparations so that it pulls the plant energies into the liquid. To work with the planetary hours, you can either use the ruling planet of the herb or the planet that is associated with the intended effect of the herb. If you plan to use the herb for multiple preparations, I suggest working with the ruling planet. At the height of the harvest season, it is helpful to make a chart of the moon phases and planetary hours for the week ahead so that you have them on hand when needed.

Prepare your sacred space by physically and spiritually cleansing the area in which you will be working. A floor sweep, a vinegar cleanse of counters, work table, and tools, and washing your hands before you craft will ensure that no negative energies or germs taint your work. You will need just a few special tools to prepare a variety of magickal preparations, including a blade for chopping, a mortar and pestle or grinder, a double boiler, a glass funnel, glass pipettes or droppers, and cheesecloth for straining.

Common Preparations for the Ritual Apothecary

SACHET: Usually a cotton, silk, or natural fiber bag containing herbs that have been chosen to work together toward a specific intention, the sachet is enchanted in the ritual space and worn on the body or in a pocket, placed in a special spot, or kept under a pillow, depending on its intention. This is also called a charm or *mojo* bag.

INFUSION: An infusion is a botanically based oil that has been infused with herbs chosen to work together toward a specific intention. Fill a glass jar one half of the way with dried plant material, and then cover it in botanical oils such as sweet almond oil, olive oil, fractionated coconut oil, or sunflower oil. Place the jar in the sun for two to three weeks in

a *solar infusion*, or heat it in a double boiler on low for a few hours and strain it through cheesecloth into a new jar, making sure to squeeze every last precious drop of magick out of the plant matter. To increase the potency, allow the herbs to infuse through one Full Moon.

FLOWER ESSENCE: A water-based remedy that contains the subtle vibrational imprint of a chosen flower, this method is useful for taking in the energies of otherwise toxic plants. After choosing the flowers based on their intuitive properties, fill a small glass bowl with spring or purified water and gently drop the flowers onto the water, blossom side up, until they cover the surface. Leave the bowl in full view of the Noon Sun for at least two hours. Then remove the flowers and pour the water into a clean container until half full. Fill the bottle to the top with organic vodka, and label it as the *Mother Essence*. From the Mother Essence, add seven drops to a 1 ounce (30 ml) glass bottle filled with vodka, which makes up the *Stock Bottle*. From this Stock Bottle, add seven drops to a ½ ounce (15 ml) glass bottle filled with vodka to make the Medicine Bottle, from which you can take a dose of up to four drops four times daily, either in water or simply dropped under the tongue.

TINCTURES AND ELIXIRS: These are alcohol or vegetable glycerin extractions of plant material. Spoon fresh plant material or dried plant material that has been ground with a mortar and pestle into a glass jar until it is one half full (if the herb is powdered, it should be covered with alcohol until it is two fingers' width above the herb). Cover the herbs with vodka, brandy, grain alcohol, or vegetable glycerin (note that elixirs are typically made with brandy and cut in half with raw honey) and place them in a cool, dark place for four to six

weeks. During this time, you should gently roll the jar between your hands once a day, chanting your intentions over the jar as you do so. For instance, if you were crafting a rose tincture, you could say something like "Love and nurturing, make your way from the petals to the potion." During the Waxing Moon, decant the liquid through cheesecloth into a clean jar and store in a cool, dark place for up to one year. Dosage will depend on the herb.

BALMS, OINTMENTS, AND SALVES: You can make solid preparations of oil infusions with beeswax (or candelilla wax as a vegan alternative) and/or plant butters. Heat the herb-infused oil with wax in a 1 part wax to 4 parts oil ratio, pour into tins or glass containers, and allow it to cool until hardened. Balms typically have plant butters such as shea, mango, or cocoa butter added during heating for a creamier texture. Balms should be tempered in the freezer until solid to avoid a gritty texture.

A WORD ABOUT ESSENTIAL OILS: Essential oils are the oils that are extracted from a plant, and they contain the "essence" or scent of that particular plant. While they can be beneficial for aromatherapeutic and medicinal purposes in ritual skincare, they are also a highly concentrated form of the plant. This can add to the energetic bang of your magickal preparations, but can also cause allergic reactions or other health issues. In this respect, it is of utmost importance that you ensure your essential oils are from a reputable source and do not contain impurities that may negatively affect your rituals.

Herbal Alchemy

Alchemy is one of the oldest sciences in the world and speaks of the ability to transform the mundane into magick. In modern tincture making, we often extract only two out of the three parts of a plant, leaving the salt behind. However, using the ancient technique of *spagyrics* to process the whole plant, we can impart the maximum amount of energy and healing to an herbal tincture, which is known as a *spagyric remedy*. In Greek, the word *spagyric* means "separate and recombine." Thus, the spagyrical process involves isolating, purifying, and recombining the three principle elements of alchemy: sulfur, mercury, and salt.

Sulfur is the soul or individualized essence. It is the volatile oil of the plant and is associated with the Fire element. The sulfur is obtained by distilling the essential oil of a freshly harvested plant. If you do not have distillation equipment, the sulfur can be extracted along with the mercury by gently heating the alcohol.

Mercury is the life force. It is the extracting liquid and is associated with the element of Water. The plant matter from the distillation of the sulfur, or dried plant matter that has been ground with a mortar and pestle, is fermented in alcohol and decanted into a tincture. Here the extracting liquid containing the mercury is called the *menstruum*.

Salt is the physical body. Associated with the Earth element, it is composed of mineral salts that are extracted from the ash of the plant. The salt is obtained by burning the residual plant matter, the

THE EMERALD TABLET

The Emerald Tablet is an ancient alchemical text attributed to Hermes Trismegistus that describes the secrets of the philosopher's stone and the concept of *as above, so below*. The philosopher's stone is the alchemical work of the *Magnum opus*, or the Great Work, and is thought to impart immortality as the elixir of life. Capable of transmuting mundane metals into gold or silver and healing illness, the creation of the stone has been pursued since ancient times. The phrase *as above, so below* means that all things are interconnected. The visible and the invisible are but the same. The universal law of the Spirit element, it pervades everything yet it exists as nothing.

ALCHEMY IS ONE OF THE OLDEST SCIENCES IN THE WORLD AND SPEAKS OF THE ABILITY TO TRANSFORM THE MUNDANE INTO MAGICK.

marc, and reducing it to a white ash. The ash is then mixed with distilled water, filtered, and slowly evaporated to obtain the crystallized mineral salts.

These three alchemical elements, the essential oil (sulfur), the tincture (mercury), and the minerals (salt), are then combined into a single bottle that now contains the whole essence of a plant in potion form. Often, the process is started on the day and planetary hour of the herb's planetary ruler and begins by calling forth the influence of the planet. Using your mortar and pestle, you then combine your own energetics with those of the ruling planet and the plant by physically macerating the chopped plant. As you grind the herb into a powder, focus on your intention and on drawing down the planet's influence into the plant. You are then ready to process the three constituents of the spagyric remedy.

Creating Your Materia Medica

As you seek the wisdom and energetics of a vast variety of herbs, chronicling your knowledge in a plant journal can be incredibly useful for future use in your craft. A *materia medica* is a collection of knowledge about plants and their medicinal and magickal uses. Your *materia medica* can consist simply of pages in your grimoire, or you can maintain a separate *materia medica* just for herbal knowledge. Here you may want to include a sketch of the plant along with all of its parts (seeds, roots), its growing habits, its ruling element and planet, magickal and medicinal uses, and the preparations that will best preserve its energetic imprint.

Magical Recipes for the At-Home Apothecary

Below you will find simple recipes for magickal preparations so that you can begin to fill the shelves of your home apothecary. If you wish to use spagyric alchemy for the elixir, please feel free to do so.

FLYING OINTMENT

To be used in rituals concerning lucid dreaming or astral travel. Best performed on the day and planetary hour of the Moon, the planet of dream journeying. Charge with amethyst.

1 Harvest and dry (or purchase dried) lavender, wormwood, yarrow, and mugwort. Grind the herbs in your mortar and pestle, focusing on your intention as you do so. Place in an 8-ounce (240 ml) glass jar and cover with fractionated coconut oil. Place the jar in a sunny window for 2 to 3 weeks or heat in a double boiler on low heat for a few hours. Strain the oil through cheesecloth into a clean glass jar and store in a cool, dark place.

2 Combine 4 ounces (120 ml) of the herbal oil with 1 tablespoon (15 ml) of beeswax (or candelilla wax for a vegan alternative) in a double boiler and heat on low until the wax has completely melted. Remove from the heat, allow to cool for 5 minutes, and then add a capful of vitamin E oil. If you like, add 10 to 20 drops of lavender and sandalwood essential oil. Pour into two 2-ounce (30 ml) tins and allow to cool until hardened. Store in a cool, dark place.

JOYFUL HERBAL FLOOR WASH

To be used to bring joy and abundance into the home. Best performed under the Waxing Moon on the day and planetary hour of the Sun to bring in positivity. Charge with citrine.

1 Blend equal parts of dried lavender, rosemary, thyme, and sea salt to fill a 2-ounce (60 ml) measurement, and steep in 4 cups (960 ml) of boiling water with fresh lemon slices for 30 minutes. Strain into a bucket. Add 1 gallon (3.8 L) of spring water, 1 cup (240 ml) of white vinegar, and 20 drops of lemongrass and orange essential oils to the floor wash. As you mix, say your intention aloud: "Bring joy and abundance to this happy home."

2 With intention, begin mopping at the farthest point from the door and make your way toward it, chanting your intention until you finish. As the floor dries, notice the brilliance it imparts on the room.

HEART ELIXIR

To be used in rituals for mending the heart. Best performed under the Waxing Moon on the day and planetary hour of Venus to bring in healing and love. Charge with rose quartz.

1 Harvest and dry (or purchase dried) rose petals. Fill an 8-ounce (240 ml) glass jar one half of the way with the whole petals. Pour 4 ounces (120 ml) of brandy into the jar and top with 4 ounces (118 ml) of raw, local honey. Close the jar tightly and roll gently between your hands to mix. Place it in a cool, dark place for four to six weeks, occasionally mixing with intention. You many chant "Open heart, whole heart" as you mix.

2 Decant and strain the elixir through cheese-cloth into a clean jar, being sure to press down on the petals to extract all of the liquid. Bottle and take two to three drop-perfuls one to two times daily as needed.

FLORIDA WATER ALTAR SPRAY

To be used prior to rituals to cleanse your sacred space. Best performed under the New Moon on the day and planetary hour of the Sun to bring in fresh energy. Charge with selenite, citrine, or clear quartz.

1 Fill a stock pot halfway with distilled water and steep a few handfuls of freshly harvested cedar leaves, rose petals, and thyme with peels of orange and lemon, whole cloves, and cinnamon sticks for 1 to 2 hours or until the rose petals are blanched. Occasionally stir with intention while chanting "Cleanse the energy, sacred water."

2 Strain and, once it has cooled, add 1.7 ounces (50 ml) of vodka for preserving and 20 to 30 drops of an essential oil blend that includes bergamot, lavender, lemon, and rose.

3 Bottle and spray on your altar, magickal tools, or hands and feet before a ritual to cleanse and protect against negative energy. Store in a cool, dark place.

CHAPTER 9

DIVINATION, DREAM MAGICK & PARTING THE VEIL

Woven delicately into the gossamer fabric of the aether is the entirety of the human experience. We reach into this enigmatic material when we seek the future, and from it we receive guidance from the spirits that speak the language of their element. Knowing this, we might think that our lives are predestined, that tarot cards tell our fortune, and that the lines on our palms lay out our paths. But destiny is only a probability.

It is subject to free will and our ability to change our lives in real time. The knowledge that comes from across the veil tells us what our future will be if we do not veer from our current path. And so, when we look to the etheric realm for answers, we do not ask it for a prediction of an unchangeable future. Instead we ask it what we need to change to reach the future we foresee for ourselves. Thus divination, spirit communication, and dream magick are but different ways to acquire knowledge and empower our magick.

Preparing Your Energetic Body

Accessing the etheric realm, whether through our own ability to connect with the Spirit element or by spirit communication, requires a level of preparation beyond that required for the rituals we have previously performed.

Energizing Your Etheric Body

Beyond ensuring that your magick has a clear and strong conduit through which to travel, you must also work to energize it. Quarter calling, ritual oils, potions, teas or herbs, talismans, and sigils can all work to empower your magick and guide you to the etheric plane. Crystals, too, are excellent allies for divination, particularly because it is an art that calls for extreme focus. Amethyst vibrates at the level of the third eye, which is the gateway to higher consciousness, and thus is a powerful ally for divination. Labradorite, lapis lazuli, and moonstone are all helpful in enhancing intuition, psychic powers, and lucid dreaming, and can be made into a grid or worn on your person (see How Crystals Shape Our Magick on page 116). Most importantly, focusing on your question and silencing any external noise is the key to receiving the information you desire.

Protecting Your Etheric Body

In opening yourself up to the language of the universe, it is wise to be cautious of the state of your etheric body. There are negative energies that scour the veil for loose tethers and when they pull a little bit of you in, that bit may not return in the same condition. Riding the hedge, the liminal boundary between this world and the next, is not a party trick and should not be taken lightly. If you are feeling out of balance, energetically low, or emotionally raw, it is best to seek divinatory guidance from another divination reader until you are back on your emotional feet, so to speak. Before beginning any divinatory work or any such work in which you will be accessing the Spirit element, you will want to cleanse and protect both your sacred space and your astral body. Although I often recommend acting intuitively when it comes to your personal practice in witchcraft, protective circles are absolutely necessary when it comes to divination and spirit communication. Here, too, I prefer a physical barrier of black salt as well as a metaphysical barrier of light.

Timing

The Full Moon is the most potent time for the high-vibrational work of accessing the otherworld. According to the *The Key of Solomon*, the planetary hours of Saturn, Mars, the Moon, and Mercury are best for divination and spirit communication, with the ideal time in the hour of Mercury with the Moon in an airy sign.

The seasonal festivals of Beltane and Samhain are liminal times when the veil is thinner and spirits can easily cross into our world, and vice versa. On these nights, the energy required to pierce the veil will be much lower and the transmission of universal knowledge will flow more freely.

WITCHES' BLACK SALT

❧

To be used for warding off unwanted spirits. Best performed under the Dark Moon under the planetary influence of Mars.

1 In a mortar and pestle, grind ash from your fireplace (or activated charcoal) with black pepper until it resembles a fine powder. Add 1 ounce of the powdered ash to 2 ounces (57 g) of sea salt with a pinch of baking soda (to absorb moisture) so that the salt is still black once all the sea salt has been added.

2 Place the black salt in a fireproof vessel and sprinkle with a pinch of angelica. Burn the angelica as it lies on the salt and allow it to smolder over the salt until it is reduced to ash. Once cooled, mix all of the combined angelica ash with a few black tourmaline chips.

3 Sprinkle the black salt across the thresholds of your sacred space and use it to cast a circle of protection around you before divination or spirit communication.

4 After completion of the ritual, bury the used black salt in the earth since it retains the negative energy it has absorbed.

Divinatory Tools:
From Cartomancy to Tasseomancy

In divination, we seek the knowledge of the unknown from the records of the entire past, present, and future, which are kept in the etheric realm. We can access this information simply by opening our third eye and learning the language of the Spirit element, or we can ask the spirits close to the veil to translate for us. As a practitioner of natural witchcraft and a mystic, you can decide on the method you will use to receive the information. In this section, we will discuss the tools that translate this knowledge into something we can understand.

When divining, keep in mind that time as we know it does not exist in the etheric plane. Here on Earth, we occupy three spatial dimensions. But in the etheric plane, time is also a spatial dimension, with the past, present, and future all accessible at once, like rooms in a house. The information that you receive may not make sense right away. It might speak of something that will happen in the future or something that has happened in a past life. If you do not understand its relevance from one method, try to clarify its meaning with another.

Cartomancy

Cartomancy is a divination method that uses a deck of cards to explore the unknown.

TAROT: Occult tarot card reading originated in the mid-1700s and has continued to be a favorite with esotericists ever since. Tarot decks have seventy-eight cards that are separated into two Arcana: the *Major Arcana*, which has major influences on our life, and the *Minor Arcana*, which has minor influences on it.

The Major Arcana consists of twenty-two trump cards that tell the story of the Fool, who makes his journey to the World in what is known as The Fool's Journey. If there is one card you should become familiar with, it is the Fool, because he represents all of us at the beginning of our journey to our higher selves. To me, there is no better representation of the Fool and our life's journey than Pamela Colman Smith's illustration for the Rider-Waite tarot deck. Here the Fool is getting ready to embark on his journey. His bag is packed with all that he needs; he has a carefree spring in his step; he is looking toward the sky and his higher self, and he is dressed in fancy, flowery garb. He has a white rose representing innocence and a companion who will guide him along the way. He is ready for his journey. But he is still a fool. He represents us both at birth and at the beginning of our journey toward our higher selves.

The bag that he carries is too light and has yet to be opened. His clothing is impractical at best. The flower? It symbolizes naïveté. And the little dog is warning him to look down at the ground

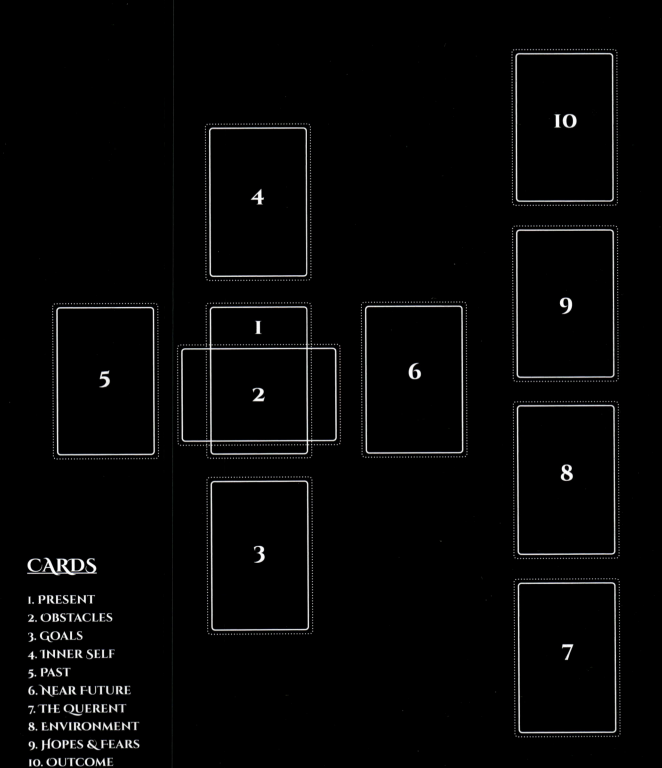

CARDS

1. PRESENT
2. OBSTACLES
3. GOALS
4. INNER SELF
5. PAST
6. NEAR FUTURE
7. THE QUERENT
8. ENVIRONMENT
9. HOPES & FEARS
10. OUTCOME

MAJOR ARCANA IN TAROT

0	THE FOOL: Start of a journey, innocence, enthusiasm
1	THE MAGICIAN: Creativity, manifestation, imagination
2	THE HIGH PRIESTESS: Wisdom, intuition, practicality
3	THE EMPRESS: Fertility, nurturing, abundance
4	THE EMPEROR: Authority, stability, reason
5	THE HIEROPHANT: Tradition, religion, conformity
6	THE LOVERS: Love, trust, harmony
7	THE CHARIOT: Overcoming adversity, success, willpower
8	STRENGTH: Courage, strength, action
9	THE HERMIT: Introspection, solitude, searching
10	WHEEL OF FORTUNE: Fortune, fate, cycles
11	JUSTICE: Reason, honor, righteousness
12	THE HANGED MAN: Pause, respite, surrender
13	DEATH: Transformation, endings, unexpected change
14	TEMPERANCE: Moderation, harmony, patience
15	THE DEVIL: Malevolence, binding forces, temptation
16	THE TOWER: Sudden change, downfall, abandoning old ways
17	THE STAR: Hope, optimism, purpose
18	THE MOON: Intuition, inner self, worry
19	THE SUN: Success, vitality, joy
20	JUDGEMENT: Repentance, judgement, rebirth
21	THE WORLD: Completion, fulfillment, triumph

because he is about to step off the edge of a cliff. But the Fool is not a fool because he is a bad person, or because he is doing something wrong: He simply has much to learn. In the Major Arcana, the Fool is numbered 0, the start of your journey to the World. We are the Fool not only at birth but also at the beginning of every journey, big or small, because life itself is cyclical and knowledge is never finite. Along the Fool's Journey, we will meet many figures of inspiration and influence as we search for guidance.

The Minor Arcana consists of fifty-six cards that are divided into four suits. These are Swords, Wands, Pentacles (or Coins), and Cups. Each suit has four court cards and ten numbered cards. These are similar to regular playing cards, except that the court cards consist of a King, Queen, Knight, and Page. The four suits, like the four elements of nature, should always be kept in balance in your life. If there is an imbalance between the suits, the cards will tell you how to balance each area of your life that relates to them. When divining with tarot cards, you can consider the Minor Arcana to be associated with the elements and thus with the four parts of a person: the mind, the core self, the outer self, and the emotions.

SWORDS: Air. The Mind. Often represents struggles, conflict, or negative aspects that require action and change.

WANDS: Fire. The Core Self. Associated with energy, creativity, rapid expansion, will, and determination.

PENTACLES: Earth. The Outer Self. Associated with wealth, business, and material possessions.

CUPS: Water. Emotions. Associated with love, partnerships, emotions, romance, fantasy.

Reading the Cards

Learning to read tarot may seem daunting at first, but once you grasp the basic concepts and begin to understand the symbolism, you can read quite intuitively without memorizing what each card means. Although we have not talked about the reverse meaning of tarot cards (that is, when a card is flipped upside down in a reading), you may choose to read reverse meanings. This can be done purely by intuition, knowing that there are two sides to every attribute. For instance, the

High Priestess is known for being practical and objective, but in reverse, she might question her intuition and rely on the opinions of others too much. Or she might trust her intuition too much and not listen to others at all, thereby becoming short sighted. For greater accuracy, it is important to let the querent handle the cards either during shuffling or by cutting the deck into three while they focus on their question.

LENORMAND: Lenormand is a thirty-six-card *Petit Jeu* deck (French for "little game") based on the Game of Hope, which was a card game widely played during the late 1700s. It was named after the famous diviner Marie Anne Lenormand, who first used the deck for cartomancy. A Lenormand spread often provides the directness that tarot sometimes lacks and can be used to bring clarity to a tarot reading. There is a specific order to the cards, and they contain symbolism that is quite

TAROT SPREADS

❧

To be used in divination. Feel free to create your own intuitive spreads. Best performed under the Full Moon or during liminal times.

ONE CARD PULL: This is a quick and easy daily draw that can help you become intimately acquainted with each of the cards. Pull one in the morning to see if there is a message for you or an answer for a question you may have.

THREE-CARD SPREAD: Past, Present, Future. This spread can assist you in uncovering the path to take to address a particular issue you might be experiencing—for instance, how to overcome a creative block.

CELTIC CROSS TEN-CARD SPREAD: This spread is a deep dive into your life's journey.

CARD 1: *Present.* Represents the querent in their present position

CARD 2: *Obstacles.* Influences that are crossing the querent

CARD 3: *Goals.* The querent's ideals within the present situation

CARD 4: *Inner Self.* The querent's subconscious influences

CARD 5: *Past.* What happened in the past leading to the present position

CARD 6: *Near Future.* What is about to take place

CARD 7: *The Querent.* The perspective or approach of the querent to their present position

CARD 8: *Environment.* Relationships and influences of others

CARD 9: *Hopes and Fears.* Inner emotions and secret desires

CARD 10: *Outcome.* The culmination of all the events and influences if everything occurs as indicated in the rest of the cards

LENORMAND SPREADS

To be used in divination for direct answers or predictions. Best performed under the Full Moon.

TWO-CARD SPREAD: Offers insight into what might occur on a given day or insight into a question.

THREE- OR FIVE-CARD SPREAD: Offers deeper insight into a question, perhaps regarding a relationship or a promotion, for example.

GRAND TABLEAU: The Grand Tableau can tell you the entirety of your life's journey based on the universal knowledge of your current path. It uses all thirty-six cards laid out in one of two ways, of which the 9 × 4 spread is the simplest, consisting of four rows of nine cards. Like astrology, each position in the spread relates to a house or area of your life. The houses follow the order of the cards across the rows and relate to the card that is placed in the house, similar to the way in which a zodiac sign relates to the house it is in on your natal chart. The cards are read in relation to each other in various directions and groupings until a complete picture is obtained. While a Grand Tableau can often take hours to explore, the outcome is quite rewarding.

intuitive: The Rider is associated with the arrival of news; the Clover with luck; the Ship with travel, and so on. More than most cartomancy methods, Lenormand is literal and predictive, meaning that it speaks more to the actions that will occur around you than to the paths you can take to alter your course. The most important rule of Lenormand is that the cards are never read alone, only in relation to each other. Lenormand cards represent not only actions but timing as well, and in this way, you can predict when an event might occur.

ORACLE CARDS: Oracle cards are an intuitive cartomancy method based on symbolism or the power of word association. They are often read in conjunction with tarot cards or used during rituals as a focal point.

Chiromancy

Palmistry, or palm reading, is a divinatory method that reads the hands for details about the life's journey. Likely originating in India and brought to Europe and beyond by the Romani, palmistry is an art form that requires a bit of study and a lot of practice. When studying the hand, there are a number of factors that can be considered.

HAND: The Left Hand represents your ancestral line and shows you your life's path, which was laid out at birth according to universal knowledge. The Right Hand represents how the choices you have made have changed your destiny.

SHAPE: The shape of the hand is usually classified by element and can thus relay the characteristics of a person based on their elemental attributes.

EARTH: Square palm with short fingers

AIR: Square palm with long fingers

FIRE: Rectangular palm with short fingers

WATER: Rectangular palm with long fingers

LINES: There are seven primary lines on the palm that are examined in a reading. The quality of each line can tell you how a person has approached that area of their life or how it has been affected by their choices. The deeper and straighter the line, the more positive the outcome. Timing is also indicated along the lines and is numbered in five- to ten-year increments from a point of origin to pinpoint the age of significant occurrences.

LIFE LINE: Span and quality of life. Any breaks indicate times of great change

HEAD LINE: Thought and communication

HEART LINE: Love, relationships, and emotions

RELATIONSHIP LINES: Number and length of important romantic relationships

SUN LINE: Outer self, recognition, success

Mercury (Health) Line: Overall health and state of digestive system

FATE LINE: Course of life. Any breaks indicate change by outside sources

HILLS: Hills or mounts represent the first nine planets (including the Sun and Moon) and can affect lines based on their planetary attributes.

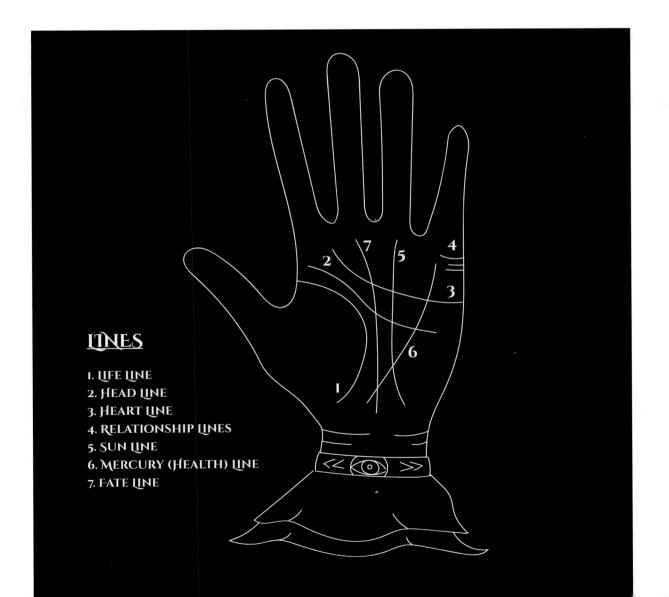

LINES

1. LIFE LINE
2. HEAD LINE
3. HEART LINE
4. RELATIONSHIP LINES
5. SUN LINE
6. MERCURY (HEALTH) LINE
7. FATE LINE

Dowsing

Along with Lenormand, dowsing is one of the more direct divinatory tools. A board, cloth, or paper is marked with answers like "Yes," "No," or "Maybe," as well as a number line and the alphabet, if desired. Then a question is asked and either a knife with a rounded handle is spun until it stops on an answer or a pendulum is held over the dowsing board between the thumb and the forefinger until it begins to swing on its own toward an answer. In either method, it is important to focus on your question while chanting it out loud.

CROW OR MAGPIE AUGURY

Counting crows or magpies in the sky is a folkloric method of *augury*, the practice of reading omens based on the flight pattern of birds. In ancient Roman times, an augur would observe these *auspices*—signs presented by the birds—to foretell the future. Also called ornithomancy by the Greeks, this method of reading omens made its way into the superstitions of Europe in the 1600s. There are many versions of the popular "counting crows" rhyme to help you remember your omens, but Michael Aislabie Denham's version in *A Collection of Proverbs and Popular Sayings Relating to the Seasons, the Weather, and Agricultural Pursuits* published in 1846 was one of the earliest versions that accounted for up to seven magpies or crows: "One for sorrow, Two for mirth, Three for a funeral, Four for a birth, Five for heaven, Six for hell, Seven for the devil, his own self." A more modern version has been popularized in children's nursery rhymes and amends the lyrics as so: "One for sorrow, Two for joy, Three for a girl, Four for a boy, Five for silver, Six for gold, Seven for a secret, Never to be told. Eight for a wish, Nine for a kiss, Ten for a bird, You must not miss."

Runology

The runic alphabet, called *futhark*, originated with the ancient Germanic people of northern Europe and the Nordic countries. While there are three main varieties of script, early Germanic Elder Futhark is the most common rune script used in modern witchcraft. It contains twenty-four letters that can also be read in reverse. Although runes can be used as powerful talismans in spells and ritual work, they are often used for divinatory purposes in spreads and rune casting. They offer guidance much in the way that tarot does, in that the information received is up for interpretation and subject to free will.

RUNE READINGS: To be used for divination. Best performed under a Full Moon.

SINGLE RUNE READING: Offers insight into a question.

THREE RUNE READING: Past, present, future. Offers deeper insight into a question.

CASTING RUNES: A small handful of runes are tossed out of the bag and read in relation to each other.

ELDER FUTHARK RUNES

NAME	SYMBOL	LETTER	IMAGE	MEANING IN DIVINATION
Fehu	ᚠ	F	Cattle	Money, power, control, abundance
Ūruz	ᚢ	U	Ox	Health, vitality, energy, success, physical strength
þurisaz	ᚦ	Th	Thorn or Giant	Defense, protection, reactive force, instinct
Ansuz	ᚨ	A	Divine	Creation, vision, insight, communication, wisdom
Raidō	ᚱ	R	Wheel	Travel, journey, choosing the right path
Kenaz	ᚲ	K	Torch	Knowledge, vision, second sight, power of fire
Gebō	ᚷ	G	Gift	Relationships, connection, honor of others
Wunjō	ᚹ	W	Joy	Joy, good news, harmony, fellowship
Hagalaz	ᚺ	H	Hail	Difficult or destructive situations that will ease
Naudiz	ᚾ	N	Necessity	Willpower to overcome reliance, resistance
Īsaz	ᛁ	I	Ice	Block until change is made
Jēra	ᛃ	J	Year	Cycle of life, peace and bounty in nature
Eihwaz	ᛇ	Ei	Yew Tree	New beginnings, purpose, goals, motivation
Perþ	ᛈ	P	Dice Cup	Memory, hidden knowledge, free will
Algiz	ᛉ	Z	Elk	Defense, protection, shield, ward
Sōwilō	ᛊ	S	Sun	Clarity, success, positive changes
Teīwaz	ᛏ	T	Creator	Success in legal matters, justice, honor
Berkana	ᛒ	B	Birch Tree	Birth, fertility, new beginning, growth, renewal
Ehwaz	ᛖ	E	Horse	Change in a positive direction, progress
Mannaz	ᛗ	M	Mankind	Self as part of whole, society, cooperation
Laguz	ᛚ	L	Water	Water, flow, psychic abilities, dreams
Ingwaz	ᛜ	Ng	Fertility	Protection of home, family, love, hearth
Dagaz	ᛞ	D	Day	Security, stability, balance, awareness, awakening
Ōþila	ᛟ	O	Home	Inherited or ancestral wealth, homeland, heritage

Scrying

The ancient Egyptians gazed upon oil in a vessel to foretell the future, but the art of scrying has been practiced in some form by every culture throughout history: By the first century CE, Druids gazed into crystal balls, the glowing orbs later brought to Western society by the Romani. While there are many methods of scrying, the process to reach the deep meditative state necessary for gazing is the same. To enter a trance state, begin by gazing at a single point on the scrying surface until your eyes begin to lose focus and a mist comes across. Keep gazing until the mist clears and silhouettes rise out of its depths. Allow the subconscious to take over as your conscious mind fades away.

WATER GAZING (HYDROMANCY): Gazing upon a pond or other still body of water is best done at high Sun or during a Full Moon. If you like, you may also pour naturally sourced water into a vessel and scry upon the surface with candlelight.

FIRE AND SMOKE SCRYING (LYCHNOMANCY): A bonfire, fireplace, the flame of a candle, or tendrils of incense smoke can reveal dark shapes in the flames that dance with their revelations. For this purpose, you may want to use casting herbs such as mugwort, cinquefoil, clary sage, wormwood, and jasmine. Note that several of these herbs are psychoactive and contain thujone, so should be used with caution.

CRYSTAL GAZING (CRYSTALLOMANCY): A polished crystal or crystal ball can be chosen so that the nature of the question corresponds to the attributes of the crystal type. For example, if your question is about love, you might choose to gaze into a rose quartz sphere.

MIRROR GAZING (CAPTROMANCY): A scrying plate made of polished obsidian or a black mirror can be viewed under moonlight or in the light of a candle. To craft a black mirror, paint the back of a mirror with black paint until it is opaque. Between the mirror and the frame, draw the algiz and laguz runes in chalk (see chart on page 153), or include powdered herbs such as mugwort or eyebright. You may also adorn the frame with crystals such as amethyst, labradorite, or lapis lazuli to strengthen the connection with the Spirit element.

Tasseomancy (Tasseography)

Trade routes in the 1700s brought tea and tea leaf reading from its roots in China to Western occultism. However, tasseomancy has been used to tell fortunes in many other cultures. The Middle East regions read coffee grounds, while the French look for patterns in wine sediments. Reading these patterns and symbols explores a person's future according to their current path. While reading styles are left to the diviner's imagination, there are a few basic tenets of tasseomancy to which most diviners adhere.

TEA LEAF
READING

1 Tea leaf reading should be performed with loose tea only. Smaller leaves like black tea, nettle, peppermint, or lemon balm all work wonderfully; however, you should feel free to choose a leaf-based tea blend that resonates with the querent. Fine, powdered tea as found in teabags should not be used.

2 The cup should be white so that the symbols can be clearly seen. A saucer should also be selected, but the pattern is not important as it will simply be used to allow the cup to dry. You may use the astrological or printed cups, but they are not necessary. The tea is to be drunk and swirled in the nondominant hand, as this will activate the subconscious. The querent should focus on their question throughout.

3 When a tablespoon of liquid is remaining in the cup, the sediment should be swirled three times in a clockwise fashion until the liquid reaches the rim, tilting the cup a bit, if necessary. The cup should then be covered with the saucer, inverted, and placed on the table. Allow the sediment to dry for two to three minutes. Spin the saucer until the handle is facing the querent and turn the cup back upright.

4 To read the tea leaves, start at the handle (which represents the querent) and make your way around the cup in a clockwise spiral from the rim to the bottom. This is the timeline from the present to the distant future. The symbols nearest the handle will represent the present. As you move around the rim, the symbols will become less influential and have more of a passing effect on the querent. As you make your way around and down into the cup, you will be traveling along the querent's life path until you reach the very bottom. This is the distant future and is thought to be the querent's life's purpose. Whether or not the symbols are well-defined will mark whether the event foretold by the symbols will be positive. If they are shaky or ill-defined, then it may mark a time that brings difficulty.

5 Symbol dictionaries, although tempting, should not be used. Of all the divinatory methods we have discussed, tea leaf reading is considered the most personal, interpretive, and intuitive. Symbols should be interpreted according to your own subconscious and the universal knowledge you pull into your craft. Here, becoming familiar with numerology as well as traditional symbolism can be helpful, but you should not have one hand in the dictionary and the other on your cup. Let your intuition guide you through the interpretation.

Spirit and Animal Guides

Spirit and animal guides are metaphysical creatures that are meant to guide you through the etheric realm on your journey toward tapping into the universal knowledge. Although you may call on them to guide you in rituals and spells, they remain in the spiritual realm, which is where you must meet them. They can be based on a real person or creature, a god, goddess, or angel, or something that appeared to you in a vision. My spirit guide appeared once at a gate while I was looking for a lost object. In looking deeply at her, I saw that she was a crone, more ancient than anything fathomable, but immortality had graced her with flaming red hair and a svelte body that lives off the wilds. She wears a tattered emerald dress, and she knows every animal in the forest and every blade of grass in the misty fields.

Never smiling, she can command the fog. Her hands are long and bony, but they point with a knowing wisdom that I trust wholly. While the appearance of your spirit or animal guide does not matter, they should have within them the map of the entirety of the etheric plane, and you should feel comfortable following them. Animal guides will present themselves based on their attributes and your intentions. For instance, if your intention is to grow your intuition and wisdom, you might call upon the owl. Animal guide selection is an intuitive process: Compare their habitats and characteristics to the qualities with which you would like to connect.

CALL UPON YOUR SPIRIT OR ANIMAL GUIDE

To be used for summoning your spirit or animal guide in a lucid dream state.

1 Create a sacred space around a comfortable area. After cleansing the space with sage, burn a cone of incense, such as frankincense and myrrh or cedarwood, on a charcoal disc or in a censer. Ensure that the room is completely dark except for the burning tip of the incense.

2 Focus on your intention and gaze at the incense until the smoke fills your vision and your gaze slips from the conscious to the subconscious. Visualize being in a field: All around you is the smoke, a thick fog that you cannot see past. You hold your hand in front of you, but you cannot see it. As you walk slowly forward, the dark silhouette of a large, gnarled oak comes into view on your left side. You make your way around it as the fog engulfs it once again. You continue walking until the post of a wrought iron gate comes into view. The fog clears around the gate and there, standing beside it, is your guide.

Animal guide selection is an intuitive process: compare their habitats and characteristics to the qualities with which you would like to connect.

Lucid Dreaming and Astral Travel

Although there are many arguments for the separation of lucid dreaming and astral travel, this book adheres to the belief that, through the Tibetan technique of WILD (wake induced lucid dream), we can achieve astral projection. Lucid dreaming is the art of remaining in conscious control over the exploration of the subconscious or dream plane. Here you can do things that you may be fearful of doing in real life: A surgeon can practice a surgery or a performer can sing on stage.

You can also work with your subconscious to alter your real experiences and empower yourself in the waking world. For instance, you could plant a seed of intention or search for lost objects. You are asleep during most lucid dreaming techniques, having gained consciousness only after you enter the dream realm. If you are in a conscious meditation (that is, you never fall asleep) and your astral body leaves your physical body, then you have projected into the etheric plane. In witchcraft, we commonly refer to this experience as *riding the hedges*, and it is a key practice for the hedge witch who mingles with the spirits there. The riding experience always begins in the same room where your body is and ends with a deliberate effort to return your consciousness back to your physical body. Along the way, you may meet your spirit guide or many spirit guides as well as animal guides. It is especially important here, where time anomalies allow you to leave one century and enter

PLANTING A SEED

Planting a seed in a lucid dream can help you empower yourself in the physical world and is useful for building confidence and self-esteem, gaining strength in fighting addiction, overcoming past traumas, and encouraging healthy habits.

1 Begin the visualization meditation for finding your spirit guide, but this time, when the fog begins to clear, it reveals to you a secret spot where you can plant your seed. This could be under a tree, in the middle of a deserted field, behind an abandoned cemetery, or anywhere that you feel comfortable planting it. Remember to tell no one, either in the dream plane or in real life, where you planted your seed.

2 Say an incantation over the seed once it is buried: "As you grow, so does my willpower over ____," or "As you grow, so does my confidence."

3 Return at least once a week to nurture the plant and watch it grow as you feel your strength and empowerment grow in the physical plane. When you visit your plant, you may water it or sing to it, but remember that some attributes, particularly confidence, can grow too large and overshadow the other parts of your personality, so careful pruning may become necessary over time.

another, to recognize that etheric information is not linear. As you ride, remember that you are there to seek knowledge and gain insight into your practice so that you may empower it.

WILD FOR ASTRAL PROJECTION

1 Place a broomstick by a window in your bedroom. Lie on your back, close your eyes, and gaze into the blackness of your eyelids or your mind's eye. If you like, massage Flying Ointment into your third eye, between your eyebrows. Focus on your breath, slowly breathing in through your nose and out through your mouth. Binaural beats or a sound machine may help you further relax and tune out thoughts.

2 The onset of the *hypnagogic state* (the point between wakefulness and sleep) will often begin with vibrations, shaking, sounds, or the appearance of color patterns. I often hear what I can only describe as "a skipping orchestral symphony." Acknowledge and engage with these— track them, think actively about them—to ensure you do not slip into unconscious sleep. Here you may begin to silently chant a mantra like "I am conscious. I am awake." At this point you may experience sleep paralysis and feel your etheric body still locked to your physical body. You may become aware of a presence, like the pervasive Old Hag, or heavy breathing and footsteps. If this happens, it is not safe to astral project. Exit your state immediately.

3 If able to move on, visualize that the broom handle hovers above you. Reach for it and begin to lift your astral body out of bed. Peer down and see your physical body below you. You are now free to move about the etheric plane. Leave through the window on the broom and allow the Spirit element to move you along.

4 When you are ready to return to your physical body, visualize it and you should instantly return to it. If you experience trouble with reentry, look for the silver cord that connects your etheric body with your physical body and follow it until you reintegrate.

Parting the Veil and Speaking with Spirits

The veil is the liminal space between this world and the etheric plane. The etheric plane is made up of vibrations and contains the knowledge of all that has happened, is happening, and will happen. This includes the wisps of spirits that remain from previous lives and lives to come. Often, if they have something to say or want something, they will approach us. But we can also initiate communication using tools, just as in divination. Remember that the spirits that dwell close to the veil remain there for a reason. There is something in the physical realm that they desire.

It may be a benevolent reason, such as watching over a loved one, but it could also be a desire for vengeance. These wisps of spirits do not contain the entirety of their being and so reason and empathy are often not present. The remaining energies of a person in the spirit realm are the strongest attributes of that person in life, and not all people are inherently good. Cleansing, grounding, and protection rituals should precede any attempt to communicate with the spirit world and should include a strong focus on the types of energies you are reaching out to. Parting the veil is best done during a time of transition, such as the solstices and equinoxes, but contacting the spirits can be done at transitory times of day such as sunrise or sunset, or at areas of transition such as where the forest meets the field or the land meets the sea. From here, you may follow the guide for Energizing Your Etheric Body (see page 142) and include calling the quarters as well as deep meditation or lucid dreaming prior to contacting the spirits. Dancing and chanting are particularly effective in opening the portal.

Spirit Communication

There are many tools used to communicate with spirits, but they all work in the same way. Divination, dowsing boards, spirit boards, seances, and channeling or invocation are all merely tools that bridge the language barrier between the vibrations of the aether and our human senses. After you have entered a meditative or trance state, begin to call the spirits. "Benevolent energies from across the veil, make yourself known." As you look for signs, remember that these spirits do not speak our human language. Through vibrations, they may speak through a flickering flame, an unintelligible sound, or the shaking of an object. As always, if you feel a negative presence, immediately cast the spirit away and close the portal. For this purpose, it is helpful to have a black tourmaline wand for casting off unwanted energies. Once you acknowledge the presence of a spirit, you may ask it questions. Although you may be tempted to find out about its life or identity, do not travel down this path. They will tether themselves to you as you feed the memories onto which their shreds of self cling. Instead focus on the fact that their existence in the etheric plane allows them access to all knowledge of the past, present, and future. Use this to empower and inform your practice and to imbue your life with purpose. Once you have asked all of your questions, cast the spirits away, thanking them for their immense knowledge, and close the portal: "Thank you, spirit, for sharing your wisdom. You will cross the veil back to the spirit plane. This portal is now closing." Finish by cleansing the area with sage smoke and salt water washes.

DIVINATION, DOWSING BOARDS, SPIRIT BOARDS, SEANCES, AND CHANNELING OR INVOCATION ARE ALL MERELY TOOLS THAT BRIDGE THE LANGUAGE BARRIER BETWEEN THE VIBRATIONS OF THE AETHER AND OUR HUMAN SENSES.

CHAPTER 10

PERSONALIZING YOUR PRACTICE

Now that you have empowered yourself with all the knowledge this book has to offer, you can do the important work of personalizing your practice to make it your own. There are many ways to incorporate your own personal power into witchcraft, but we will touch on a few significant ones.

Sigil Crafting

Sigils are magickal symbols that are enchanted with unique purposes that can empower your craft. Mostly considered to be a tool of *chaos magick*, in which the practitioner imparts their power into an object, sigils are spells in and of themselves. When crafting a sigil, you weave magick into an intention and create a symbol that can be used as a talisman. Crafting a sigil is an incredibly personal part of your practice and it must be created by you, for you. No one can craft a sigil for you. The power is in the energy *you* put into it and what it means to you. Although the process is simple, the result is nothing short of magickal.

SIGIL CRAFTING

1 Write your intention down on a piece of paper. In this example, we will craft a sigil for use during divination rituals: "My Third Eye is Open."

2 Now remove all the vowels until you are left with the consonants: "M Y T H R D Y S P N"

3 Remove the duplicates until you are left with the base symbols: "M Y T H R D S P N"

4 Now rearrange the base symbols into a single glyph by combining all the letters into one. Spin the paper as you combine them, building one letter off another. Feel free to change the size and shape of the letters and to make them as simple or as ornamental as you like.

5 Activate the sigil by burning it in a candle flame, watching any emotional or creative work that you put into it burn away as it merges with the Spirit element and envelopes you in its intention. Beliefs on whether sigils have a place in the physical world differ, and so you may choose to leave this particular sigil to work its magick in the aether forever, or you may write it down in your grimoire to be used again.

Creating Your Grimoire

A grimoire—which is sometimes called a Book of Shadows, particularly in Wiccan traditions where a single book of magick has historically served entire covens—is a journal in which you can store all the knowledge you have gained in your craft. It can include spells, rituals, seasonal and astrological observations, herbal magick and alchemy, lore, techniques, personal sigils that you have used, talismans, and anything else you have learned in this book and made your own.

Although you can certainly buy a blank grimoire, crafting your own can weave a protection spell into the book itself so that it always remains in the right hands. You may also choose to write your grimoire in the Theban alphabet, a sixteenth-century system of writing based on a cipher of the Latin alphabet. Also known as the *witches' alphabet*, this substitution of letters is thought to protect your magical writings from others. Cleansing and charging your grimoire like any other magickal tool should be an important part of your ritual. One day, you will look at your grimoire and be pleasantly surprised at how much you have poured into your craft.

The Theban alphabet as published in Johannes Trithemius's Polygraphia in 1561

CREATING YOUR ALTAR

An altar is a sacred location that provides focus for rituals and magickal workings. Although altars are highly personal and often intuitively designed, there are a few steps that can help you create them with ease. The first step in building an altar is to determine its purpose. Whether it is to honor the season, worship a deity, or stand as a spell shrine, the altar you create will provide a sacred space in which to work your magick. Finding a location for your altar is the second step and may depend on the altar's purpose. For instance, if you wanted to construct an altar to call upon the Earth element, you may want to locate it outdoors. In the third step, you will want to choose a foundation for your altar. A tree stump, a small table or fireplace mantle, or even the rim of a bathtub can be the perfect place to create your altar. The fourth and final step is to fill your altar with symbolic artifacts and magickal tools that will assist you in your craftwork. Offerings of gratitude can also be made to thank the energies at work for empowering your space.

Familiars

While familiars may be shapeshifters or forest dwellers, they can also be lifelong pets. The important thing to remember about taking on a familiar is that you feel an intuitive connection with them and nurture your relationship in a reciprocal way. The role of a witch's familiar is to protect, assist, and guide the witch in their practice. They have a close connection with nature and can thus convey the energy of the Spirit element to you, further empowering your magick.

Witchcraft and the Family

Bringing witchcraft into the family can create a sense of connection and bring empowerment to the home. Celebrating the seasonal festivals, communing in nature, and participating in bonding rituals can attune you to each other as well as to the land on which you live. This type of nurturing creates an unbreakable cycle that ties you to each other as you come to rely on the deepened well of magick the bond creates. If there are children in your life, you will see that they find great joy in celebrating the seasonal festivals, baking magick (especially for faeries and other nature spirits), exploring nature, and the sparkly magick of crystals.

CELEBRATING THE SEASONAL FESTIVALS, COMMUNING IN NATURE, AND PARTICIPATING IN BONDING RITUALS CAN ATTUNE YOU TO EACH OTHER AS WELL AS TO THE LAND ON WHICH YOU LIVE.

Crafting in the Southern Hemisphere

If you live in Australia or anywhere in the Southern Hemisphere, you will want to make adjustments to several concepts introduced in this book.

Seasons
Because the seasons of the Southern Hemisphere differ by six months from those of the Northern Hemisphere, both the seasonal Full Moons and festivals should be adjusted accordingly. For instance, while the Northern Hemisphere celebrates Yule in December, the Southern Hemisphere celebrates it in June.

Circle Casting
Deosil (sunwise) is counterclockwise in the Southern Hemisphere because of the way the Sun moves across the sky. Similarly, widdershins (anti-sunwise) is clockwise.

Cardinal Directions
In the Southern Hemisphere, the cardinal direction of North is Fire, while South is Earth.

Moon Phases
The Waxing Moon will appear bright on the left in the Southern Hemisphere, while the Waning Moon will be bright on the right.

CHAPTER 11

RITUALS, CHARMS, & ENCHANTMENTS

The following rituals can be personalized to suit your individual needs or practice. Before you begin each ritual, take the time to choose a space that you feel safe in, and arrange your space in a way that will facilitate your ritual. Before beginning your ritual, be sure to have a clear focus and to cleanse the area and your magickal tools with herbal smoke, spray, crystals, or light. Use magickal timing, invoke spirits or angels, evoke the four quarters, or just envision yourself surrounded by a powerful aura of energy. Use the tools that this book has given you to empower your magick in the way that best works for you.

Banishing and Protection Spells

HEX-BREAKING BOX

To be used in transforming the energy of a hex or curse. Best performed under a Waning or Dark Moon under the influence of Mars.

1 Obtain a rectangular box (a shoebox would work) and a mirror that is roughly the same size as the upright end of the box. Over the mirror, incant "Bind the energy that harms" until the hex has transferred to the mirror. This will be apparent when the mirror begins to feel heavy and the reflective surface darkens.

2 Now attach the mirror with the bound hex to the inside of one end of the box with glue. Spread black salt along the bottom of the box. In front of the mirror, in the salt, stagger four iron nails upside down. In front of the nails, in the salt, place a black tourmaline standing point, followed by a rose quartz standing point. Space them so that the black tourmaline is in the middle of the box and the rose quartz is at the far end (the opposite end of the mirror).

3 Begin your ritual in meditation and form an image of the curse or hex you want to break. It is helpful here if you imagine it as a shadowy entity.

Hold that image in your mind as you sit at the opposite end of the box and gaze into the magick mirror. Visualize the hex swirling in the mirror, waiting to unleash its negative power on you. It is okay to feel frightened, but remember that the mirror is binding the hex's power.

4 As you incant "I release you," visualize the wisps of the dark entity seeping out of the middle of the mirror, trying to make their way to you as they wrap themselves around the nails, as if they were becoming lost in a maze. As they make their way through the nails, the black tourmaline draws their dark energy in like a magnetic portal. Incant "I transform you" as you visualize the hex traveling through the black tourmaline and emerging as a beam of light that shines on the rose quartz. Incant "I release you" as you visualize the light filling the heart and being released into the universe as a warm, glowing light that spreads joy and positivity.

5 Bury the black salt in the earth, cleanse the crystals and mirror, and retain the hex box for future use.

CUTTING THE CORD RITUAL

To be used in releasing yourself from a negative person. Best performed under a Waning or Dark Moon under the influence of Mars.

1 Choose a cord. Black is the preferred color, as this is a tie that binds you to a negative energy. Write your name and the name of the person you are cutting the cord with on separate pieces of paper (or use photographs). Roll each up and tie one to either end of the cord.

2 Dress a black candle with rosemary and powdered copal by sprinkling them around the wick with intention before burning. Draw the cord taut, lower it into the flame, and burn the cord in the middle.

3 As the cord separates, envision the piece of your heart that was tied to the other person being returned to you and reconnected with your heart. Envision your heart whole and glowing. Picture the other person whole as well. There is nothing of you left inside them. The purpose of this ritual is to free both of you from the ties that bind. Burn the two ends of the cord (with the names or photos still attached) separately and bury the ashes in opposite directions.

PSYCHIC ATTACK

A psychic attack is a feeling of anxiety, depression, sleeplessness, or heaviness that is brought on by another person's ill intentions or negative energies. These energies often arise from the person's unacknowledged shadow self and cast darkness on your psyche. If the attack is intentional, it may be a result of a hex or a curse. But even if it is not, the effect is often equally debilitating. This shadow dampens your spirit and your magick, but it also drains your vessel of its ability to host positive energy. If you have ever been around someone who projects misery, you will be able to recount the exhaustion and stress you feel after the encounter. There are many ways to protect against psychic attack, such as cleansing with herbs and crystals, bathing in light, expanding your aura, and using dream work, but one of the most effective ways to dispel psychic attack is by cutting the metaphysical cord with the person or thing that has brought you negativity. In this way, you are cutting the tie that binds and returning each end to its rightful owner.

Candle Magick

ELEMENTAL QUARTERS CANDLE

To be used in evoking the elements before a ritual. Can be performed under any moon phase and planetary influence.

1 In a small cast iron pot, follow the instructions for basic candle making in the House-Blessing Candle (see below). Do not add essential oils, however; just pour the wax into the pot and allow it to harden almost completely but so that the surface is still melted. Separate a tablespoon of each of the following herbs on your work space: rosemary (Fire), lavender (Air), rose (Water), and sage (Earth), and, if you like, have essential oils for each at the ready.

2 While the wax is still slightly melted on the surface, use your ritual utility blade to carve the top of the candle into quarters with two lines that cross in the center (skip over the wick). In the lower right corner, sprinkle the rosemary; in the upper left corner, the lavender; in the upper right corner, rose; and in the lower left corner, sage. As you do this, chant "Fire, Air, Water, Earth." Now, in the same order, drop one to two drops of the matching essential oil on top of the herbs and repeat the elemental incantation.

3 Allow it to cure for 24 to 48 hours. Place the candle on your altar with each of the elements facing their direction (Fire: South, Air: East, Water: West, and Earth: North). Light before a ritual to evoke the power of the elements in place of calling the quarters.

HOUSE-BLESSING CANDLE

To be used in cleansing your home of negative energy. Best performed under a New Moon under the influence of Saturn.

1 Prepare a clean 8-ounce (240 ml) jar by winding a cotton wick around a dowel and placing the dowel horizontally over the mouth of the jar so that the wick touches the bottom of the jar in the center. Gently heat 16 ounces (0.5 g) of soy wax flakes in a double boiler. Remove the wax from the heat and allow it to cool for 5 minutes. With intention, grind a few leaves of dried sage and cedarwood to a powder in your mortar and pestle and set aside.

2 Blend 20 to 30 drops of sage and cedarwood essential oils into the melted wax and stir. Pour the wax into the jar and allow to cure at room temperature for 24 to 48 hours. Work magick on the candle in your sacred space, and as you dress it with the powder you crafted, chant "Cleanse and bless this space. Protect it from harm and allow only joy to cross its thresholds."

3 Place the candle in the main entry to your home. As you light it, visualize that the negative energy is being cast off and that a bright light is emanating from it until it fills the room.

Healing Rituals

HEALING AN AURIC TEAR

To be used to repair a hole or crack in the auric body. Best performed under the Full Moon under the influence of the Sun.

In meditation, gently explore your aura, focusing on any dark spots you may come across. Note where and how wide they are and explore where they may have come from. Once you have identified and acknowledged the dark spots, begin the healing process. With a clear quartz tower, run a beam of light longitudinally over your body, visualizing that, as the crystal passes over the dark spots, it seals them with light until they seamlessly blend with the rest of your aura. After all of the dark spots have been sealed, take a salt or fresh water bath (or bathe in moonlight) to complete the healing process and energize your newly repaired aura.

DISTANCE HEALING POWDER

To send healing energy across a distance. Best performed under the Full Moon under the influence of the Sun.

In your mortar and pestle, grind a tablespoon each of dried agrimony, elder flower, and thyme to a powder. As you grind, visualize that the person you are sending healing energy to is happy, vibrant, and full of vitality. If you know the source of their illness, focus on the healing of that area. Cup your right hand and spoon the powder into it (the right side is the giving side of the body). Outside, with the direction of the wind, blow the powder out of your hand. As it travels through the air, visualize that it is making its way to the receiver via the Spirit element and working to heal them. Before performing this spell, be sure to ask for permission from the receiver.

MEMORY CHARM BAG

To be used for building or retaining memories. Best performed under the Waxing Moon under the influence of Mercury.

In a small bag, combine dried eyebright, rosemary, and peppermint with a hematite tumble (tumbled stone). Tie the bag shut so that there is a loop on the end. Through the loop, run a cord that is long enough to wear around your neck and under your shirt. Squeeze the bag and say, "Help me remember all that I need." Charge it under the Waxing Moon or the noon Sun for a few hours before each use. Use as needed during exams, speeches, or in times of anxiety to retain memory and composure over the mind.

BEFORE YOU BEGIN EACH RITUAL, TAKE THE TIME TO CHOOSE A SPACE THAT YOU FEEL SAFE IN AND ARRANGE YOUR SPACE IN A WAY THAT WILL FACILITATE YOUR RITUAL.

Love and Attraction Spells

BEAUTY WATER

To be used to increase your radiance, inside and out. Best performed under a Full Moon under the influence of Venus in spring or early summer.

1 Place rose quartz and clear quartz at the bottom of a glass pitcher and fill it with freshly collected spring water. Collect petals from flowers such as roses, peonies, hibiscus, and lotus, and, as you do so, thank the flower for its attributes: "Thank you, rose, for your gentle nurturing."

2 In view of the Full Moon, gently drop the petals into the water until they cover the surface. Allow the water to absorb the radiant energy of the Full Moon for an hour or two, then decant into a glass jar with a dropper or spout.

3 Every morning and evening, splash some of the beauty water into your cupped hands and pat your skin with it. Allow the water to air dry and feel the radiant beauty from the Moon and the flowers seep into your skin.

OPEN HEART RITUAL

To be used to heal and open your heart after loss. Best performed under a Waxing Moon under the influence of Venus.

1 Anoint yourself and dress any candles or magickal tools with an Open Heart Oil made from 1 ounce (30 ml) of rose-infused sweet almond oil blended with 5 to 7 drops each of rose, vanilla, and cardamom essential oils.

2 Sit or lie down and close your eyes. Breathe. Let the scent of the oil fill your nostrils as you focus on your breath. Breathe deeply and slowly in and out, imagining a rosy light shining down onto you and entering your lungs through each breath. As you exhale, breathe out everything negative that has ever happened to you. Let go of those negative thoughts and experiences. Once you begin to feel only the vibrations of positive energy inside you, place a piece of rose quartz over your heart and take a long, deep breath. Picture the light entering your heart through your breath. Turn your focus to the rose quartz. Feel the love and joy enter your heart as this powerful healing stone works its magick to repair and open your heart. Picture your heart whole and open and radiating light.

3 If you used a candle, burn through it completely over the course of the next week or so to continue to heal your heart. For the next week or so, carry the rose quartz crystal with you and anoint yourself head to toe with the Open Heart Oil (paying special attention to your heart chakra), until the oil runs out.

Luck and Prosperity Spells

PROSPERITY SACHET

To bring good fortune and prosperity to the home or business. Best performed under a Waxing Moon under the influence of Mercury or Jupiter.

Spoon equal amounts of dried alfalfa, spearmint, and chamomile flowers into a yellow or beige muslin or cotton sachet. Include a lucky coin if you have one and tightly tie the bag. Hold the sachet in your left hand, squeeze it, and say, "Grow my fortune and bring me prosperity." Focus on your wealth increasing through benevolent means. Then, place it in your safe or money box, or in the cash register or safe at your place of business.

LUCK AMULET

To be used for bringing good luck to the bearer. Best performed under a Waxing Moon under the influence of Jupiter.

Select a medium-sized green aventurine tumble and hold it in your left hand. Focus your intention on it, visualizing the luck that it will bring you. Bury the stone in the earth (the element associated with luck and growth) for a full 24 hours, sealing in the intention. Carry the stone in your left pocket when you head out to seek your opportunity.

HONEY JAR

To be used for sweetening deals in business or finances. Best performed under a Waxing Moon under the influence of Mercury.

1 Select a small glass jar with a lid. Be sure to cleanse it physically and metaphysically before use. Decorate it with crushed pyrite, coins, gold chain or wire, or anything else that represents money to you.

2 Write your petition in ink on a small piece of paper, being careful not to lift your pen as you tie the name of the opportunity and your intention with your own name. For instance, you could write "Bank of the universe, grant a small business loan to Luna Bell."

3 Sprinkle a bit of dried mint on the paper and fold it twice. Place the petition with a few flakes of gold leaf into the jar and cover it with honey. To charge or recharge the honey jar, place a tealight dressed with mint, chamomile, or basil essential oils or herbs on top of the jar and allow it to burn through completely.

Resources

BOOKS

A History of Witchcraft: Sorcerers, Heretics, & Pagans by Jeffrey B. Russell and Brooks Alexander

Book of Shadows by Gerald Gardner

Buckland's Complete Book of Witchcraft by Raymond Buckland

Cunningham's Encyclopedia of Magical Herbs by Scott Cunningham

Encyclopedia of Crystals, Revised and Expanded by Judy Hall

Grimoire for the Green Witch by Ann Moura

Seventy-Eight Degrees of Wisdom: A Book of Tarot by Rachel Pollack

Star Power by Vanessa Montgomery

The Herbal Apothecary by JJ Pursell

The Only Astrology Book You'll Ever Need by Joanna Martine Woolfolk

The Witches' Almanac

CARTOMANCY DECKS

Tarot

Rider-Waite Tarot Deck
by Pamela Coleman Smith and Arthur Edward Waite

Russian Tarot of St. Petersburg
by Yury Shakov

The Linestrider Tarot
by Siolo Thompson

The Wild Unknown
by Kim Krans

Lenormand

Pixie's Astounding Lenormand
by Edmund Zebrowski

The Original Lenormand
from the original "Game of Hope"

The Seeker's Lenormand Deck
by Skullgarden

CRYSTALS

Energy Muse

www.energymuse.com

Moonrise Crystals

www.moonrisecrystals.com

Rock Paradise

www.rockparadise.com

HERBS & APOTHECARY ITEMS

Bulk Apothecary

www.bulkapothecary.com

Mountain Rose Herbs

www.mountainroseherbs.com

Starwest Botanicals

www.starwest-botanicals.com

RITUAL & WITCHCRAFT ITEMS

Crow Haven Corner

www.crowhavencorner.com

Light of Anjou

www.lightofanjou.com

The Coven's Cottage

www.thecovenscottage.com

Wicked House Merchantile

http://wickedhousemerchan.wixsite.com/
wickedhouse

Acknowledgments

In writing a book about my life's journey though witchcraft, it seems nearly impossible to thank everyone who has played a part. First and foremost, I must thank the online witching community in which I have found both a circle and a home. You all have boundlessly supported my craft and journey and remain ever curious and bursting with magick and for that, you are by far my biggest inspiration. Next I must thank my son, Colton. Without his inquisitive nature and astounding observation of the world around him, I would not always see the things that dance in the shadows and play in the light. I thank my husband, Matt, for being a sounding board and for affording me the space and time to work on my craft. I thank my mother and father, Judy and Chuck, for giving me the freedom to explore myself and all that the world has to offer (even if it meant not questioning the "spooky" altar in the corner of my high school bedroom). I thank my brother, Michael, for helping me through the rough times and believing in me, even when I did not believe in myself. I honor my grandmothers, Olga and Roberta, for instilling a sense of individuality and for imparting the knowledge that there are realms beyond our own. Thank you to my aunts, Theresa and Carol, who have always encouraged discussions of all things strange at family parties. And of course my lovable uncle Dan who envelopes everyone he meets in an invisible (and actual) bear hug. In both honing my craft and writing this book, I would be lost without the insight and friendship of my sister witch, Becki from Cattail Apothecary, who never ceases to be there even when a barrage of messages come her way at inopportune times. I, of course, must also thank my editor, Jill, who acted as a source of support and motivation while writing this book and, although she may not know it, often acted as a muse thanks to her brilliant vision and eloquence in writing. The entire Fair Winds team was instrumental in shaping my thoughts and knowledge into a proper book. Thank you to Megan and Elizabeth for polishing the words and helping the journey to make sense. Thank you, Nyle, for keeping a pulse on everything and connecting the dots. Thank you, Anne, for your design know-how and art direction. And thank you to the design team for putting it all together. Thank you to the spirits who translate the knowledge from the otherworld and my ancestors who gave rise to my magick. Finally, thank you to the immense and beautiful world around us; nature, who with its own enigmatic design of intricately working parts, imbues life with mystery and magick at every turn.

About the Author

Since the mid-1990s, Anjou Kiernan has sought the magick that resides within us and the natural world. At an early age, she toiled in potions and herbal remedies, explored tarot and the realm of spirits, and began a lifelong grimoire that would ultimately lead her down the path of sharing her craft with the community. From her childhood spent in the woods and later settling on a magically minded homestead in the rolling hills of rural Maine, she has cultivated a craft based on her own observations of nature and continued her spiritual journey through the hedges. Named as one of Refinery29's "Magical Women on Instagram You Really Should be Following," Anjou thrives on sharing her lifelong exploration of witchcraft and cultivation of magickal spaces.

Anjou holds a Bachelor of Arts in Biology with a minor in Anthropology and has enjoyed many extracurricular courses in history, art, ecology, botany, and literature. She enjoys painting, writing, gardening, reading, antiquing, conserving and exploring nature, and being a mama to the most magical little boy.

Index